"Terry Cole-Whittaker dares to believe that you can allow yourself to be physically beautiful and abundantly prosperous while pursuing the ineffable goals of spiritual advancement. For my money, that's terrific!"

—Lisa See, *Emmy Magazine*

"In allying self-help and human-potential philosophies with spiritual value, Cole-Whittaker obviously practices what she preached!"   —*Booklist*

WHAT YOU THINK OF ME IS NONE OF MY BUSINESS

TERRY COLE-WHITTAKER

BERKLEY
New York

BERKLEY
An imprint of Penguin Random House LLC
penguinrandomhouse.com

ISBN: 9780593333075

Oak Tree Publications edition / 1979
Jove mass-market edition / April 1988
Berkley trade paperback edition / December 2020

Printed in the United States of America
ScoutAutomatedPrintCode

Cover design by Olivia Braito

*I dedicate this book to my spiritual partner,
my most beautiful, talented, brilliant daughter,
Rebecca Austin Cole-Wiesehan*

"The fault, dear Brutus, is not in our stars,
But in ourselves . . ."

JULIUS CAESAR

I, II, 140–41

CONTENTS

1

POWER! YOU ALREADY HAVE IT

This is a book about power and how you can use it to *be* what you want to be, to *do* what you want to do, and to *have* what you want in life.

The unsettling fact is that, though each of us is born with this power, there are often times in later life when we seem headed downhill. One purpose of this book is to explain why this happens and why failures, both personal and material, are unnecessary and, in fact, unnatural.

The power that each of us is born with is a part of God, the spiritual aspect of our being, which is perfect. This power is a creator, or generator, of energy that is either *potential* or *kinetic*. Potential energy is passive energy, energy that is stored, waiting to be used. Kinetic energy is active energy, energy that is being used. As active energy, this power is neutral and may be used to create sickness, loneliness, poverty, crime, or war—or good health, wealth, peace, friendship, happiness, and fulfillment.

God has given us what some call free will, but what I prefer to call the option of *choice*. We have the choice to use our power positively or negatively, constructively or destructively.

"If that is so," you may ask, "why on earth would anyone choose the negative? No one would consciously make such a choice." And that's the point! Most of our choices are made *unconsciously*. It is another purpose of this book to teach you how to heighten your consciousness, your self-awareness, so that you can choose *consciously*.

The mechanism by which this energy becomes implemented is our mind, our mental attitudes, which, in turn, determine our belief systems, the way we perceive things. As the power is implemented—as our ideas take form, if you will—they become the reality in our lives, the reality of failure or the reality of success.

Think of your mind as the mold or blueprint that determines the shape the power takes, the form in which it expresses itself. This mold or blueprint is made up of your beliefs which, in a sense, are your memories and interpretations of very early life experiences or even prenatal existence. Unfortunately, we misinterpret many of these early experiences and bury these misinterpretations in our unconscious mind, where they become the basis for the beliefs that cause us so much trouble later in our lives.

And it is not accidental that we make these misinterpretations because, from the moment of birth, we are surrounded by other people who are imposing their misinterpretations upon us. They usually do so unconsciously because they, too, are not aware of how the power and the universe work. Because we get so caught up in trying to please these people, we spend a large part of our time worrying about what they think of us. So it is that these mistaken belief systems, with all of their attendant misery, are handed down from generation to generation.

Fortunately, our minds are designed so that we can change

them, and it is the central purpose of this book to show each of us how we can break the vicious circle of mistaken beliefs that presently go from parent to child and, in turn, to parent.

The marvelous thing is that the universe is designed so that you can be joyful, abundant, fully self-expressed, loving, and loved. The game of life is rigged in your favor, and the power is within you to change your life. It has always been there, but you must learn to accept it and to use it. One caution: only *you* can do it. This book can show you *how*, but the responsibility for acceptance and implementation is *totally yours*.

The principles are simple, for the rule of life is that ideas create forms or, put another way, that what you believe creates your reality. Simple? Yes! Easy? No! Yet, there are people right now who, through the application of these principles, are transcending their lives and becoming an inspiration to others seeking the way.

As you look around you, notice that no two people have identical lives. Some people seem to have it all: life goes their way. Others struggle and never seem to get their act together. Is it just luck or an act of God that disease and loneliness are "dished out" to some while others receive health and happiness? You may not have discovered it yet, but life is not "fair." Yet life is "just." Your life is in your hands. The power is there. The potential is there waiting for you to direct it.

Now, I'm not talking about some kind of light positive thinking. I don't want you to settle for some relative improvement in your life. I'm asking you to settle for no less than a total transformation of your life. It is ignorance that encourages us to settle for the relative good rather than the absolute. My intention is that you will be transformed and begin to live in Heaven on earth now, as has been promised by Jesus and illumined prophets of other religions.

The first truth I want you to accept is that you are already a complete person, with nothing missing. That's the way God made you.

The second truth is that you are a creative being. That is your nature, and you're always creating.

The third truth is that you create from your beliefs about God, yourself, and life in general.

The fourth truth is that you have made decisions about yourself, others, and life that were once conscious decisions but have become unconscious ones and yet continue to direct your decisions and to determine the quality of your life.

The fifth truth is that the universe is totally supportive and cooperative. It says "yes" to your ideas, to both the good ones and the bad ones. It says "yes" even to an idea that will destroy you. So, no one is coming along to save you. Only you can do that.

There's the story of the man who fell into a deep hole and yelled for someone to throw him a rope. When it finally became apparent to him that no rope was forthcoming, he grew tired of waiting and got out by himself. What I'm getting at is that the same power that traps you also frees you. You have the power, and you've always used it. You have no choice over that. The power flows continually and will be used, no matter what. You *do* have a choice as to *how* you use this power.

Your transformation depends upon conscious choices. And your conscious choices depend upon your increased awareness of yourself, upon your willingness to practice the art and skill of self-observation. Begin to stand back from yourself and observe your thoughts, beliefs, reactions to people, to those who push your buttons and to those who don't. Observe your body reactions. Notice when you are tense or relaxed. These are messages from your body, and you will learn to understand them. Observe the results in your life and recognize that the physical universe doesn't lie. Accept that you can only reap what you sow.

As you begin to observe, try to do so as a nonjudgmental observer. That's not easy, but you can be nonjudgmental with practice. You'll probably notice that you are more negative than you thought. Try not to worry, but continue to observe. The other steps will be revealed when appropriate in later parts of this book.

One of the biggest obstacles we create in our lives is our resistance to change. Most of us combat change from the day we are born until the day we die. Knowing that change is inevitable doesn't stop us from fighting it. We want stability everywhere and think that's the way to security. We want all of our friends, our lovers, our jobs to remain the same. That way, we think, we'll be safe.

In this book you will learn that, when you are at one with God, you can quit resisting change. You will learn to accept that all expressions of God are dynamic and that, consequently, various aspects of ourselves and our lives are always changing. In this book you will learn to be change's beneficiary, not its victim. You will learn how to avoid driving yourself crazy anticipating how you're going to handle situations before they happen. You will learn not to fear what others may think of your actions. You will learn that happiness is simply choosing and accepting what is going on in your life, for when you know that God, not others, is your source, you have the choice to move into life assertively and to work with change. You will learn to let go and allow God to support you.

For many, the notion of such a relationship with God is uncomfortable. That's because many of us have been taught that God is fearsome, angry, retributive, and revengeful. Yet all of the spiritual leaders—Jesus, Buddha, Lao-tzu—brought us the essential message of love and its power. It is difficult to imagine a loving God wanting us to be sick, poor, or unhappy. It's through our ignorance of the Spiritual Law, of God's love, that we bring the miseries of life upon ourselves.

As I indicated above, we overcome this ignorance and change our mistaken belief systems by developing a heightened consciousness, an acute self-awareness. At the end of the succeeding chapters of this book, you will find Self-Awareness Strategies and Exercises. Each group of exercises is keyed to the particular problem area discussed within that chapter. These exercises are there, not just for a single reading, but as a point of reference to which you may return repeatedly as problems arise in your life. In this way, you will be able to open your mind and allow yourself to grow, to enjoy full self-expression, love, and abundance. You will become a willing channel for the power you are born with.

Elsewhere in this book, you will learn that one of the reasons our creativity often fails us is because we do not carry our ideas far enough. You will find, following the Self-Awareness Strategies and Exercises in each chapter, three Affirmations. These Affirmations will help you make certain that you do carry your ideas far enough.

And, now, I will repeat to you the warning I always give to the newcomers in my seminars and my congregation: "Self-awareness will be dangerous to you. You will discover that your life is in your hands and that it's God's will that you have what you want."

2

ABUNDANCE IS YOUR RIGHT

Your belief system creates your reality, and there is no other law. Beliefs are the very foundation of your life. Your beliefs are based on decisions you made about yourself and about life at the time of your conception and birth and in response to later experiences. And because of your misinterpretation of these experiences, many of your beliefs are mistaken. These mistaken beliefs simply are not nurturing and actually cut you off from the supply of life and its opportunities.

One such mistaken belief is the *belief in scarcity*, the belief that there isn't much and that what there is, is running out. The person who holds this belief sees life as a pie with just so many pieces. If you get a piece of the pie, there is one less slice for others. Or if they have the slice you want, too bad, it's gone. If you succeed, someone else fails. If you're prosperous, somebody else must be poor. There isn't enough money. There isn't enough love. There isn't enough appreciation. There isn't enough success or attention. There are not enough jobs, mates, and on and on. It's as though life were a seesaw! If I'm up, you're down. Or vice versa. With this belief system, you can't have any *more* because there simply isn't enough to go around. So you must protect and defend what you have, take what someone has, and prevent others from getting.

I recall a young man who came to me with a desperate career problem. His father owned a drugstore, which had been owned by *his* father. When the young man was preparing to go to college, his father told him: "Go ahead and get your education, but remember, you belong here in this business. It's in your blood, and you'll never succeed anywhere else."

The son explained to me that he didn't want to work in or run the drugstore, but he didn't believe there was anything else out there for him. Nevertheless, after he graduated from college, he tried a number of jobs and failed in each. Finally, in desperation, he gave up and went to work with his father in the drugstore.

The father said: "I'm glad you finally saw the light. I was right all along. I know more about you than you do about yourself." The fact was that the son was miserable in the drugstore. He felt defeated and gutless. At this point, he sought counseling.

Through counseling the son gained insight into his belief system. He had bought the belief system of his father, that there was one slice of pie left. That slice was a job in his dad's drugstore. In counseling, he discovered his fear that, if he succeeded in anything else, he would betray his father and lose his love and approval. He loved his father so much that he was willing to give up his own happiness for him. Thus, his life had become one of compromise, which worked for no one.

Counseling revealed that he was acting from a belief in scarcity. So he changed his personal law from "I can only succeed in my dad's drugstore" to "I am a capable, worthwhile person, and I am able to be fulfilled, successful, and prosperous in any job I choose." He accepted that there were plenty of jobs and right situations out there for him and plenty of opportunities. He quit the drugstore, struck out on his own, and in a couple of years had become a very successful accountant. Initially, his father had difficulty accepting his son's independence. But because of the son's willingness to tell the truth, to do what he wanted to do, and to still express love for his father, he gradually gained the father's acceptance and increasing respect. Later, the father confided that he, too, had wanted to leave the drugstore when *his* father was alive but had lacked the courage to do so.

Through your belief in scarcity, you make yourself a slave to the idea that there's only one job, only a few friends, only one place to live, only a couple of options, just enough money, only one possible answer or solution.

I recall a woman, a well-to-do divorcée, who came in for counseling. She was forty but looked sixty. She was over-weight. Her hair was mousy and her face, lined. Her feeling of self-worth was so low that, when she walked into my of-fice, I felt as if the aliveness had been sucked out by a vacuum cleaner. She told me that her life wasn't working, that nothing was going right.

"What are you doing?" I asked. "How are you participat-ing in life?"

She said, "What can I do? No one seems to care, and there's nothing to do, anyway."

"Nothing to do" means that the pie plate of activities and fun is empty, and life is one big blank. "What would you like to do today if you could do anything you wanted?" I asked.

She paused. "Well, I would like to go to the beach," she said.

"Great! When are you going to the beach?" I asked.

"How can I? Nobody will go with me," she replied.

"How many people have you asked?"

"Two," she replied. "They are all too busy."

"Do you realize," I said, "that there are four billion people on this planet, and you're letting the last two you talked to run your life?"

Here is the pie again. This time it's the people pie. Despite the abundance of people to draw from, you will hang on to the relationship that isn't happy or fulfilling. Options galore are always available; but if you are operating from a personal law of scarcity, you won't open your mind to anything else. Therefore, your prison is of your own making.

You see, the mind is a success mechanism. Because of its duplicating nature, it will motivate you successfully to create your beliefs into real situations. The subconscious is like a computer: put garbage in, get garbage out. If you affirm over and over that "no one my age can find a job," then the machine, in essence, says: "That's right. There aren't any jobs for you." You cancel out all those jobs that are—or could be— good for you. And you will be deservedly out of work or in an unfulfilling work situation that you can't tolerate but feel you must put up with.

Yet, when you live out of knowledge, love, and abundance, the world is yours. You absolutely create your own reality.

The woman with "nothing to do" was a typical example. I told her: "You can go to the beach alone, or you can walk down the street and ask, 'Anybody want to go to the beach with me?'" Clearly, she refused to take up the options. She wearily left my office, unwilling to be responsible for her own happiness, and I never saw her again.

When you rid yourself of your belief in scarcity, you'll find that you have unlimited opportunities for self-expression, un-limited opportunities for financial abundance, for jobs, for creativity, for relationships. Scarcity creates pressure, stress, jealousy, resentment. Abundance creates support, love. Man has the incredible ability to change his life. There is no limit—except that imposed by our mistaken belief systems.

I recall a woman who was sixty-five when her husband died. After his death, she was lonely, missed male companion-ship, and wanted to remarry. The first thing she told me was: "There aren't any good men." Her very words sentenced her to a life without a new mate. The words you speak become your personal laws because of the creative power of the sub-conscious. Start listening to what you say, and you will be-come conscious of what you are affirming and of the cause behind the results in your life.

"A good man is hard to find," said the widow. For her that statement was absolutely true. The widow's personal law was that there weren't any available, acceptable men. Through counseling, we set about changing that law. She realized that, if only one good man was out there, she could have him. She remarried five years ago, and I recently received a letter from her detailing her happiness with her new husband, "a good man."

There are those, of course, who will say: "But that's just one chance in a million. That's the exception, an unusual case. Besides, if everyone did that, it couldn't work because there are more women than men on the planet." Your rational mind takes over, and once again, a good idea is killed. Don't you believe it! Not everyone wants what you want. And when we realize who we are spiritually, there will be that which is perfect for each of us.

God created the universe. It's all out there, and we are its caretakers. And if we keep using the same principles that created the universe, we shall continue to enjoy abundance—of both love and prosperity. But we needlessly avoid the positive use of these principles because of our mistaken belief systems. Abundance of all life is yours. Be open to it.

You see, your subconscious or unconscious mind is an accumulation of early *conscious* interpretations. Perhaps your parents experienced financial difficulty at the time of your birth and were anxious that you might be a burden. They really wanted you but were torn with anxiety over whether they would have enough money to support you. Because babies have a very high degree of consciousness at the moment of birth, you picked up their fear and belief in lack. Your consciousness was: "Well, here I am and nobody wants me. I am a burden, and there isn't enough money to take care of me." Or, "My being here depresses my parents." That was, of course, not a completely correct interpretation, for your parents did want and love you. But you misinterpreted their anxiety and tucked it away in your subconscious where it could haunt you for the rest of your life.

Because the mistaken interpretation first occurred in consciousness, you have to bring the unconscious events that caused it back into your consciousness to discard it. There are various avenues for bringing misinterpreted events up to the level of consciousness. Later in this chapter, I shall outline some awareness procedures that will help you correct the misinterpretations that led to your belief in scarcity.

Even as you seek to bring misinterpretations into your consciousness, you will be aware of their persistent nature. Most of our misinterpretations—though not all—came from our parents who, in turn, got them from *their* parents. It's like the biblical saying about the iniquity of the fathers being visited upon the children. What it really means is that the parents suffered a lack of self-love, and the original sin meant their separation from God, which is the separation from the abundance of everything in life: love, pleasure, happiness. Self-hatred, self-denial, self-doubt—all are the consequences of the belief "I'm not worthy." To be unified with the loving source is to accept that "I and the Father are one and I can enjoy His perfection." But through absorption of inaccurate belief systems, you lose the consciousness of abundance and, in so doing, deny your divine heritage.

We forget—or maybe many of us never knew—that *thoughts are things*. Through your thoughts (or ideas, if you prefer), you create the action that produces the results. Your state of mind creates your behavior, the way you talk, the way you walk, the way you write. It also creates what you have—your abundance or lack of it. If your thoughts are that others love you, support you, and respect you, that's what you'll experience.

Unhappily, most of us allow others to determine who and what we are. We decide who we are by the way we are treated and thought of by others. We become so concerned about being judged that we perform poorly, make mistakes, or perhaps always try to live up to someone else's expectations. We become our own worst critics. Yet, if you believe in your own self-worth and in the availability of opportunities, you are the captain of your own ship and the master of your own destiny.

If the belief in scarcity persists, no matter how much money you have, you'll still feel impoverished, materially and spiritually. Underneath it all, you'll still feel an uneasiness, an insecurity, the need to take, to stockpile, to hoard. And you will be driven by the fear that "disaster is inevitable" or that "something this good can't last" because "it's too good to be true." And then your wealth, relationships, or success will create pressure.

What I'm talking about throughout this book is a transformation of the self. When *you* are transformed, your life will automatically be transformed. The Bible says: "But seek ye first the kingdom of God, and his righteousness; and all these things shall be added unto you." That kingdom of God is the sense of love you experience, the sense of certainty that you are in tune with a greater power, that life has rules guaranteeing you all you want, and that you will always be provided for. "Seek ye first the kingdom of God . . . and all these things shall be added!" Sounds simple. And it *is* simple.

But most people turn it around and try to add all the things in order to experience the kingdom, the abundance, the love, certainty, and satisfaction. They think that, if they *have* and *do*, they will *be*. The order is reversed. *Be*, then *do*, and you'll *have*. Plenty of wealthy people are still insecure. If your interest is money, you can get it—through scrupulous or unscrupulous means—but it won't be the big ticket to happiness.

The distinguished minister and counselor Emmett Fox said that, in counseling thousands of people through the years, he was often asked: "Would you rather counsel a rich person or a poor person?" His answer: "I'd rather counsel rich people because they know that money won't solve their problems." You can't convince a poor person of the truth of that. Most people, poor or moderately well-off, feel that, if they just had something or someone, their lives would work.

My message here is twofold. First, you are complete and nothing is missing. Consequently, nothing in life can add to you. Right now, where you are, you have it all and you may be blocking the good. Second, the Creator of this abundant universe is your Creator, and you function as a spiritually creative being in the same manner as your Creator. Put your energy and thoughts into attitudes and behavior of abundance and love. When you discover a belief, examine it. Ask yourself: "Who says this is true? Is this a law or only a belief?" If the belief isn't producing what you want, discard it. In its place, create a new belief, one you truly want to have produced in your world. Your belief is the context of that part of your life in which things happen. Affirm that you desire to prosper and then choose abundance of all that is important to you.

SELF-AWARENESS STRATEGIES AND EXERCISES

▓ OBSERVE

Notice how you feel about abundance. Do you feel poverty is a virtue? Do you feel that opportunities are few and far between?

How do you feel around abundant people? Do you feel that people with money are more apt to be selfish than those without? Do you welcome people with new ideas or do you feel that they are troublemakers?

How do you feel about the government? Do you look to Washington for the solutions to your problems?

How do you feel about the supply of love and material goods? Do you believe it is ample? Or do you complain that there isn't enough to go around?

■ CHOOSE

Take responsibility for what you have in your life right now. If you feel you don't have enough money, say, "I accept that, right now, I have chosen to have this amount of money." If you feel you don't have opportunities, say, "I choose to think I have few opportunities." Whatever your attitudes are about abundance, choose them, own them, admit that they are yours and yours alone, knowing that this is a step toward change.

■ GIVE UP BLAME

Don't blame yourself for the situations you have created, just accept them. And don't try to lay the blame on other people, places, and things. Judgments of "right" and "wrong" only create feelings of guilt or anger and get in the way of your growth. Love and accept yourself as you are.

■ CREATE IT THE WAY YOU WANT IT

Take time to visualize exactly the amount and kind of abundance you want for yourself. If it's greater experience of success, more love and friends, more clients or buyers, be specific about that. If it's creative ideas and opportunities, be specific about that. See yourself in abundant situations, with a beautiful home, interesting people, doing the things you want to do. Imagine how you would feel, what you would say, how you would dress. Write a detailed affirmation about the abundance you want. Read it aloud at least twice a day.

AFFIRMATIONS

1. I, _____, know that God has created an abundant universe, and I accept my generous share of that abundance now.

2. I, _____, attract to myself interesting and creative people whom I enjoy.

3. I, _____, accept that I have the right opportunities to use my creative talents.

3

BREAKING THE CIRCLE OF GUILT

Guilt, like *sin*, is a highly charged word. Mere mention of it almost always brings a negative response. There are two kinds of guilt: *real guilt* and *false guilt*. Both can be intensely painful, and either may offer you an opportunity to transcend pain and know the ultimate experience of total love and self-expression.

False guilt is that guilt which is laid upon you by others in their efforts to control you and to make you responsible for their lives. A simple example of this kind of guilt is the mother who says to her son: "Go out and have a good time. Don't worry about my being here all alone. I'm used to it." Naturally, the child feels guilty and says to himself: "I really shouldn't go out and have a good time while she's all alone." The guilt the child feels in this instance is *false guilt*. It's false in the sense that the child isn't doing anything he should feel guilty about. Doing what he wants in no way takes away from another or denies the mother the opportunity to have what she wants. Webster defines this side of guilt as: "A feeling of self-reproach from *believing* that one has done a wrong."

Real guilt occurs when you suppress another person mentally, physically, or spiritually; when you deny another person his liveliness, his natural ability, his happiness and self-expression; when you deny other persons the support they need to believe in themselves. Webster defines this side of guilt as: "The fact of having done a wrong or committed an offense." In the simple example of the parent and child, the parent was acting out of *real guilt* while the child was acting out of *false guilt* and fear. Each, of course, suffered.

I think it is clear that each of us suffers from a combination of *real* and *false guilt*. We suffer *real guilt* when we are the suppressors and *false guilt* when we are suppressed. Most relationships, unhappily, are basically created out of our insecurities and need and, therefore, rest on a foundation of fear. Most of us fear at some level that other people wouldn't be with us if they could really choose freely. Such an element of fear is felt, in some degree, by all of us. The true relationship must come from the position of: "I love and support you to be all that you are and all that you are not. I love and support myself to be all that I am and all that I am not. We are in this relationship because we choose to be and not because we have to be. I will not harm you or harm myself. Each of us is capable of being, doing, and having what we want. Each releases the other from the responsibility of being his or her source and the provider of happiness and well-being. We acknowledge that God is the source; people are the avenues. Yes, from time to time when I'm giving myself the permission to love myself, it may appear to you that you are the one who has showered me with love feelings. The reality is that the love feelings I feel when I am with you *come out of me*."

That is the nature of a true relationship. Through the fear that we might not approve of other persons—thus invalidating them and our experiences with them—we use guilt to control them. But you can't hold back another without hold-ing back yourself. Yet we extend our protective (we think) need to control others to our marriages, our parenthood, to the management of our business, and even to our schools.

Just take a look at a school you know. Notice the many rules that prohibit kids from doing this or that. It's obvious that whoever created the school system proceeded from the assumption that no one chooses to go to school: they go because they have to. Actually, if the schools were alive and had courses and teachers that sparked the kids' imaginations, you couldn't keep the kids away from school. The fact is that children want to learn and, in their early years, hunger and thirst for knowledge.

But we create schools based on the false assumption that kids don't want to learn. And if that's the idea held by the parents, the teachers, and the administrators, you can bet your life that's the idea the kids will have. They don't want to go to school, and they don't want to learn. And when they don't learn, they feel angry at themselves and others and to-tally frustrated in their efforts to know the world and them-selves. And they suffer *false guilt* which, in turn, may become *real guilt* as they aggressively fight back at the system through acts of violence or vandalism.

Because guilt—false or real—is a personal burden, it cre-ates a vicious circle. To free yourself of guilt, you lay it on to others who, in turn, give it back, and so on and on. We are intrinsically ethical. No one outside ourselves needs to pro-vide us with the consequences of our actions. We do that ourselves. We are judge and jury, and the punishment can be very severe. Mental institutions are filled with people punish-ing themselves because of religious guilt for their sexual desires and needs or guilt they feel for not having lived up to their parents' expectations. These are people made to feel "wrong" and, therefore, unloved and unworthy. Sadly, they are not aware that they are suffering false guilts that have been laid upon them.

Organized religion has created and perpetuated the belief that only the "right kind" of people will receive God's love and blessings. The trouble is that it is other people—not God—who are making the judgments about who is and what makes a "right" person.

I recall a letter I received from two parents who were unhappy with their son. They wrote that they had had all these plans for him to go to school and become a professional man. But, instead, he had gone his own way and, to top it all off, was following an Eastern religion. The father had become sick because of the son's behavior, and neither parent could understand how he could create pain and suffering in the very people who loved him so much, the very people who wanted only the best for him. The trouble was that their concept of what was best was not what the son considered best.

As I came to know this situation better, I learned that these parents had spent their entire lives trying to suppress the son, to make him fit their picture. They never took the time to say: "Let's support our son in what he wants to do." Instead, by trying to control him, they laid this false guilt on him. So if he did anything *he* wanted to do, he *always* felt guilty.

What these parents had done was to try to follow a life script imposed upon them by *their* parents and the rest of society. This script, reinforced by television and popular literature, said something to the effect of: "For you to be a good parent, your son must go to college, work in this kind of job, marry, settle down, and live in a house with a white picket fence," and so on. Now when the son didn't follow the script, the parents felt they hadn't done a good job and *they* felt guilty.

It's ironic that, even though people want to make a contribution to the well-being of others and to truly be of value, their concept of what makes a real contribution is usually erroneous. The reason is that parents are suffering *false guilt* laid upon them by others. They lay this guilt upon their children and, in the process, suffer *real guilt.* Out of their own and earlier suppression, they become the suppressors. In this manner, guilt is passed from person to person to person. The consequence is that we are always dealing with both *false* and *real guilt.* Thus, the cycle of insanity is in full force.

Because of these internally and externally imposed life scripts, we as parents are more often concerned about what neighbors and relatives think of our merit as parents than about what our kids think. The Bible says that the iniquity of the fathers is visited upon the children. I believe the word "iniquity" or "sin" misses the point, because spiritually one is a complete, perfect person. "Guilt" might have been a better word. And there is the phrase "visited upon." Any visitor is a temporary resident, remaining with you only so long as you desire. You have the right to send it home. The trick is to break the circle so that the guilts will not be passed on from person to person or from generation to generation. And it can be done.

Earlier, I said that *real guilt* provides an opportunity for us to change our fear. This opportunity comes as we seek to break the circle of guilt. To break this circle, you must first stand outside the circle and observe. Observe your feelings and your thoughts. Observe how you respond to others when you deny your own wants—and when you deny others their wants. This is just a first step, but it is a necessary one.

As long as you remain within the circle, you are essentially a machine, a stimulus-response mechanism. But outside the circle, it's possible not to respond to these negative stimuli. To move outside the circle, you must try to observe your own life and relationships as objectively as possible. You must be willing to acknowledge errors and to correct them.

It's easy to try to be objective about others' lives but not about our own. You can easily spot what other parents are doing wrong with their children. But when you try to be objective about your own life, you hesitate to look too closely for fear you won't like what you see and you'll feel even more guilty than you already do.

The first evidence that you may be breaking out of the circle comes when you can acknowledge that something isn't working in your life. If you can make that acknowledgment, there's hope. The person who says continuously "I have no problems" is usually in trouble.

When you have acknowledged that your life is not working as it could, look again at yourself and your life—objectively. You will find, first, that whatever your parents or others did or did not do, *you bought into it.* The only way they could make you feel guilty was *if you gave them the power to do so*, if you gave them the power to judge. You will observe that, if you did *what others expected*, you didn't receive the fulfillment you thought would come. When you've realized that you've given your power away, you must take it back. And the reverse is true: you must give others the right to take their power back.

Often as we seek to take our power back, we become very upset with those who have been controlling us. But remember again, you were the one who gave the power away. Try to understand that those who were controlling you were trying to fulfill their own needs, trying to gain a feeling of worthiness and fulfillment through you.

As an example of what I mean, let's go back to the parents who wrote me about their unhappiness with their son. I got to know this young man, and eventually he stood outside the circle to observe his parents. He saw that the bottom line of what they were saying was "I love you." But above the bottom line was: "I'll love you *if* you'll shape up your life. I'll love you *if* you get a better job, *if* you make more money, *if* you conform to the script I have handed you."

But most important, he saw that, for all the conditions for love that were put forth, at bottom his parents did love him and that, in their frustrations, they were trying to relive their lives through him. Some parents say to their children, in effect: "My life hasn't worked with this script, so you take it and see if you can make it work."

As this young man observed himself objectively, he saw that he really wanted to serve his parents because he loved them. He wanted to make a contribution to their lives but, because he wasn't making a contribution by their interpretation, he felt terribly guilty. Above all, he saw that he always failed because he had not been true to himself. He was in a no-win situation. He had won neither for his parents nor for himself.

From our childhood we are conditioned to believe that the authority figures (those whom we allow to control us) are endowed with the power. They have the goodies; and if we are not nice to them, we won't get any goodies. Consequently, all around us people are giving away their power. And that means giving away the God-given ability to be free, happy, healthy, loving, magnificent people. As soon as the umbilical cord is cut, we begin our never-ending search for a way to return to the place where we were safe and secure for nine months. Possibly because of the birth trauma, we are immediately imbued with the fear that loved ones are going to leave us. Out of this fear we buy into the guilt that others would lay on us and give away our power.

If you are to transform your life (and that's what this book is about), you must observe objectively all the relationships in your life. Observe the real guilt and the false guilt in these relationships. Observe how, in your anxiety to get the goodies, you have been trying to be something other than what you are. Observe who is dishing out the goodies and keeping you from your life's desire.

Through your observations you will notice, or discover, your natural self, your natural state of magnificence. You will observe that, when others hold you responsible for the failures in their lives, they're using guilt as the weapon to hold you in their grasp. Still remaining objective, you'll become aware of when and how you use guilt as *your* tool to control others.

Your awareness of yourself and your total honesty with yourself—no matter how frightening—are the key to your freedom. I'm not saying these guilt feelings and thoughts will go away immediately. You'll probably continue to be caught up in some form of guilt for a while. But as you heighten your awareness and let go of your former mental and behavioral habits, you will develop a willingness to be, do, and have what you want, regardless of what others are going to say. You will also give them the same freedom. You will learn to judge the intelligence of what you are doing. You will be able to ask objectively the critical question: "Is what I'm doing really going to harm someone else or is it not?" You will learn to know when you have *really* done something morally wrong to another human being by suppressing him or her in some way. You can take a look and say correctly: "I'm really *guilty* of that." You will know your guilt because you will observe that you have tried to suppress another, tried to take away his or her aliveness, possessions, self-esteem, health, rights, or you have tried, in some way, to deny others their life.

As you sharpen your consciousness, you will eventually observe that the thing that is causing you to commit this act of suppression—this immoral act—is the *false guilt* that you suffer. You don't think that you're okay. And because of your belief in scarcity, you mistakenly think: "I can have it only if I get it from you. I can be okay only if you are not."

Because the universe mirrors our beliefs, the reality you get back is a duplication of your ideas about yourself and your relationships. If you think you're not okay, your reality will confirm this belief. Whatever you give out, that's what comes back. And that is why it is critically important for you to become aware of the tangle of confusion between *false* and *real guilt*. In truth, both are needless but both can be used to transcend ignorance and enable you to enter the Kingdom of Heaven here.

In the final analysis, of course, we always return to love. When you absolutely love who you are, you will have no need to suppress others. People who murder do so because they are trying to kill something in themselves. They don't like who they are. Many of our acts of suppression are little murders, attempts to kill things we don't like in ourselves.

When your belief becomes that you are already okay, that you are made in the image and likeness of God, who is your source, then you can do, be, and have what you want without limit. When you acknowledge yourself as a beautiful, loving person, you are not going to want or need something that belongs to me or to another.

SELF-AWARENESS STRATEGIES AND EXERCISES

▪ OBSERVE

Notice the situations in which you feel guilty. Notice those individuals and types of people with whom you feel resentful, angry, or guilty.

Be aware of how and when you try to intimidate others. Be conscious of your response and the response of others in these situations.

Notice what you fear. Where do you look for the source of your love and survival? Are you really willing to get what you say you want? Do you accept your good or do you somehow feel you're not worthy?

▪ CHOOSE

Be the source of your own feelings, thoughts, words, and actions. Choose to accept yourself exactly the way you are. To resist and lie about what is really happening only prolongs the problem. Notice and observe, then accept and say to yourself, "I'm choosing to feel guilty," or "I'm choosing to create guilt in someone else." Once you accept that you choose guilt, you can then choose *not* to accept it.

■ GIVE UP BLAME

Notice your own payoff in playing the guilt-anger game. Who does this game make wrong/right? You don't have to play, so what's in it for you? Use your power in a negative way, and you get negative results. Use your power in a positive way, and you get positive results. Quit making yourself and others wrong: doing so just perpetuates the negative. You write your own life script. Give up the old, create the new, and be free.

■ CREATE IT THE WAY YOU WANT IT

Take a specific situation with a specific person and re-create it in your imagination as you sit quietly with your eyes closed. Envision the location, the environment, the dialogue, and re-create your feelings, thoughts, words, and body sensations, even your fears. After the entire situation is real to you, face the worst: see just how bad it might be. Now create it the way you want it. Talk, think, feel, and behave the way you would like to. Allow your highest self, which knows all you need now or forever, to guide you. Ask for what you want, and allow others to express themselves freely. The key is to be honest with yourself. Allow yourself to experience all of your negative feelings. Then, replace them with positive feelings. Visualize them the way you want to be.

AFFIRMATIONS

1. It's perfectly right for me, _____, to be all that I am and am not.

2. I, _____, give myself and others the space to feel, think, and behave as we choose to feel, think, and behave.

3. I, _____, consciously love and foster the spirit of love in myself and others.

4

OTHERS ARE NOT YOUR SOURCE

Self-reliance depends on knowing deep within yourself that, no matter what's going on in your life, *others are not your source*. It's knowing that, while you do need other people and do choose to react with them, they are not responsible for your happiness.

People may be the avenue, the channel, through which your happiness, well-being, and prosperity flow, but they are not the cause. The source is God—your Higher Self, your True Self. You and I, each one of us, are like fountains from which love can flow. Unhappily, we often see ourselves as containers into which things are poured. But your True Self, like a clear spring, is outflowing with God as the source.

Because we think other people are the source of our good, we make them into gods. We look to our parents, children, mates, employers, and friends to give us security, abundance, and happiness. And, as we think that what we want emanates from others, we become frightened. We come to believe "they" are withholding, and we seek to placate them to get what we think we need. That's what dependence is. We manipulate and threaten others to get what we want. We really believe that, if "they" don't give it to us, we won't have it. As a result, our relationships become based upon dependence instead of upon love.

To look to others as the source of your love is to look in the wrong place, and you'll never be satisfied. You may try to find a substitute for love by insatiably seeking money, food, or possessions; but ultimately you will still feel empty and alone.

Look at the tragedy of Marilyn Monroe. She was a woman of great beauty and talent, yet she died ignominiously of an overdose of drugs. The sadness in her life came because she was not self-reliant. She did not recognize her God within. In her quest for gratification, she used her beauty, talent, and *helplessness*. But no matter how many people adored her, either as fans or as friends, it wasn't enough. She didn't know that she was the source. She thought it might be anyone or everyone else. She was begging for someone, something to fill the empty vessel of herself, never recognizing the ironic truth.

We all do that at one time or another. We beg others to fill us up. But when we are honest with ourselves, we know that it just doesn't work. It doesn't work because we are already filled with the Spirit, just waiting to be poured forth.

Marilyn Monroe was a dramatic example of the obviously dependent person. Look around you and you will see others. They can't pay their bills. They can't keep a job. Either they can't sustain a relationship or they cling to a relationship that is miserable. They snivel around, playing the poor, helpless victim.

Dependency, however, is not always apparent. It is often camouflaged. I know a good-looking, prosperous man in his early forties who seems proud of the fact that he's never been married. Perhaps marriage isn't for everyone, but this man merely goes from one unhappy relationship to another. If the woman with whom he is involved doesn't break off the relationship, he does. And he boasts, "No woman will ever get her hooks into me!" In talking with him, I discovered that his loudly proclaimed independence is a camouflage for fear. He's afraid to be vulnerable, so he hides behind what he misinterprets as his strength. His real-life actions say: "I'm afraid no woman can give me what I want. Rather than be disappointed, I just won't relate." So, he's not self-reliant—despite the appearances—because he's afraid to be open and willing to participate and share. He's dependent on his fear.

Both the obviously dependent person and the one who misuses his strength as a shield are really in the same place. They appear to be going in opposite directions, but both are coming from *lack* in their lives. Each in his different way is a manipulator. The "independent" intimidates and scares people away, while the "helpless" drives everybody crazy exploiting their compassion.

These dependency traps are built into our lives early. As babies we *are* dependent, principally on our parents. As we grow into childhood, our parents' desire to possess us perpetuates this dependency and denies us the opportunity to be self-reliant. Our parents become dependent upon us to provide the love they need and to fulfill the dreams that haven't come true for them. The unhappy consequence too often is a complex entanglement of dependency between child and parent.

It takes real courage to break out of these snarls. Courage is required because we've entangled need and love. Each of us, parent or child, is scared to death that, if the other recognizes his or her own wholeness, we won't be needed. Actually, the opposite is true. The more secure, whole, actualized, and self-reliant a person is, the more he or she is able to be sensitive and respond to the other person. True self-reliance allows love to flow.

Someone once said to Albert Schweitzer: "You must really be a loving, unselfish man to sacrifice your life helping so many." Schweitzer replied that, on the contrary, he was absolutely selfish. He explained that he was in Africa because he derived a great deal of personal satisfaction from being there and from doing what he was doing. In other words, Schweitzer was there for himself, and because of his enlightened self-interest and self-awareness, he was able to express compassion and love for his fellow man. Through this expression, he was there for everyone else, too.

Let's look again at how dependency develops. As parents we don't accept the fact that maturing is a gradual process. The result is that the child goes from birth to adulthood by a curious path. In our desire to keep children dependent— because we think their dependency proves their love for us— we don't allow them to mature gradually. We don't allow them to take small, independent steps. We don't allow them to learn from their own mistakes and successes how to handle their own lives. Instead, it's total dependence one day and complete independence the next. One day we say: "Well, you're only seventeen. You're still just a kid, so I'll make the decisions." The next day, they are eighteen and we say, "You're an adult now, so get out there and make your own decisions." In this way, we become the *source* for our children—and may remain so long past their initial adulthood.

So the child becomes mature in years, but not in emotions. The child then looks for, and often finds, a mate he hopes will fill the role of the protective parent. The new couple has children and perpetuates the cycle. The dependence of the parents is visited upon the children.

The final twist in this vicious circle is the dependency of old age. It's sort of a game called "I'm old now, so I'll lose my mind and you'll take care of me." Thus we go from dependency to dependency to dependency, from birth through adulthood and into old age without ever achieving maturity and self-reliance.

The sorrow is that each of us has sufficient God-given power to become self-reliant. In fact, we each use our power. Some of us, through lack of consciousness, use it toward sickness and helplessness; others of us, for "strengths" we can hide behind. And there are the enlightened ones who use their power within for loving, nurturing, supportive relationships. They are the self-reliant ones, the ones who are creative, prosperous, and healthy.

The marvelous fact is, however, that no matter how you misdirected your power yesterday, you can make a complete turnaround today. You can do this by expanding your consciousness, your self-awareness, and tuning into the Spirit that's an integral part of your True Self. But to use this power for your own good and self-reliance, you will have to give up two things:

1. You must give up every bit of self-hate, self-dislike, self-disapproval.
2. You must give up your obsessive need for approval from people other than yourself. These include your mate, your children, your friends, your parents, the people you work with, your neighbors—everyone.

Both of these steps are absolutely essential. The consuming fear, of course, is that, if you give up the need for approval, you won't get any. But that denies the central truth that through God you are the source. Therefore, loving yourself is the only approval that works.

I repeat that each of us can make a turnaround. This is possible because we are *designed* so that we can correct our mistakes and raise our consciousness, our self-awareness. Remember, the universe functions in an orderly manner. We can send a rocket to the moon and know exactly when it will get there and where it will land. We can predict the tides and the positions of the planets far into the future. We can do all of these remarkable things because there are laws in the universe. We forget that, as human beings, we are subject to the same laws.

When you truly understand that you are subject to Universal Law, you will see why it's possible to get what you want out of life. Unhappily, most of us don't know when we are living counter to this law.

To be self-reliant requires great courage because other people will not provide much support. A friend of mine said, "I can't be my own person in this society because no one will let me." That's very true. No one *lets* you be self-reliant: you *become* self-reliant.

You're probably thinking: "But don't we need other people?" The problem comes from the way we ordinarily think of *needing*. It's true that, at a very deep, nurturing level, we are all interdependent because we are all individual expressions of God. But we don't need other people to be ourselves.

On the surface it looks like you and I are different people. We look different, are of different sex, have different life experiences, hold different opinions and beliefs. Those are the superficial differences.

As we look deeper, we see that, although our physical bodies appear different, we function in the same way. Our cells reproduce in the same way, our organs serve the same purpose, our blood courses through the same systems, we use the same muscles when we walk, and so on. So, on the physical level, we are both different and identical.

On the mental level we are different subjectively, but identical objectively. Proof of this lies in the fact that similar new discoveries are continually being made at the same time in different places on the planet with no communication between discoverers. That's because we are all part of the Universal Mind (subject to the same Universal Law) and the same information is available to everyone. Each one of us has the opportunity to tap into this resource, the Universal God within. It's a matter of consciousness.

On the spiritual level, there is absolutely no difference at all. On this level there's *only* the element of consciousness, and it is absolute. It can't be measured as physical and mental things can be measured, because it is the First Cause from which all things come. The Spirit is absolute, and the incredible fact about our spiritual selves is that we are all connected. It is here, at this spiritual level, that our true, deep need of others comes.

There is simply no separation between our spiritual lives. Spiritually, we are all the same, and we are all one: none of us is alone. But it is the way that each of us uses our shared spiritual power and creative energy that determines who we are. It is through the various ways we *choose* to use this inherent, universal power that we create our individualities. We create different life experiences, relationships, jobs, and even different physical bodies. When you are conscious of your spiritual self and understand how it works, you are no longer controlled by yesterday's experiences and no longer fear that others won't love you.

But we can learn to use our spirit effectively. To do so we must use our minds. We must raise our consciousness and become truly aware of those things that impede the implementation of our spirit. To gain self-reliance, we must give up our dependence on people, places, and things as the source of our good. We must become conscious of the absolute Universal Force embodied in our spirit and realize that our Higher Self is the source of our good.

A miracle occurs when you become self-reliant: you no longer judge others because you are no longer trying to get anything from them. You are there only to support them in being who they are. You love yourself because you are God's creation; and when other people are in your presence, they know that you love them for who they are—and not for their actions.

When you truly love yourself, your mate has the freedom to be the way he or she is. Your children know you love them whether they cleaned their rooms or not. All of those around you have the freedom to become fully expressed beings because they know that you chose to be with them, to share your life with them, and to expand your understanding of yourself and of others. They know you support them in being all they can be. That's the miracle of self-reliance, and the rewards are infinite.

SELF-AWARENESS STRATEGIES AND EXERCISES

■ OBSERVE

Notice those times when you feel capable and self-reliant. What are you doing? Are you alone or with people? When and with whom do those feelings of self-confidence leave you?

How do you feel when you need to make a decision? Are you confident, or do you run to someone else for help?

If you're faced with the need to confront someone else, are you willing to handle it, or do you try to get someone else to do it for you?

How do you feel about people who are self-reliant? Do you encourage them or do you put them down out of a fear they won't need you anymore?

How do you feel about people who are meek and helpless? Are you more comfortable with them as they are, or do you encourage them to become self-reliant?

■ CHOOSE

Take responsibility for your situation. If you don't like to make decisions, say: "Okay, I don't like to make decisions. I take responsibility for that. I *choose* not to make decisions. I choose to be afraid. I choose to avoid confrontations. I choose to play helpless!"

Now, ask yourself: "What's my payoff in not making decisions? How do I feel I gain?" Your answer might be, "When I don't make decisions, I can avoid responsibility." Choose that, saying, "I choose to avoid responsibility." What's your payoff? Choose that. Continue until you feel you are at the core of the situation.

▪ GIVE UP BLAME

Quit blaming yourself and others! You are not wrong for not making decisions or not taking responsibility. You just don't make decisions or take responsibility. That's all. You may find you believe self-reliant people are selfish or show-offs or whatever. Do you see how these beliefs create a position of judgment for yourself and for others?

▪ CREATE IT THE WAY YOU WANT IT

Get a clear picture of exactly what you want. Visualize what self-reliance means to you. Create a picture in your mind about how you would respond to different situations. Imagine yourself making decisions without asking for another's advice. See yourself earning ample money, paying all your bills, and so on. Visualize taking care of yourself. Imagine how it would feel. Form a vivid picture of how you want to live.

Write a detailed affirmation that spells out exactly how you want to be self-reliant. Read it aloud at least twice a day.

AFFIRMATIONS

1. I, _____, am confident and trust in my ability to make responsible and correct decisions that produce success, happiness, prosperity, and health for me and others.

2. I, _____, have all the resources, time, energy, and wealth to do what I want in my life.

3. Whatever I have need of, whenever I have need of it, I, _____, attract it to me.

5

CERTAINTY OF PURPOSE

To have inner peace, love, and power, you must be certain of yourself and your purpose. Certainty about yourself means certainty in your ability to create what you want in life. Because you are basically a spiritual and complete being, you already possess the natural capability to handle your life successfully. But you must be *aware* that you are in charge of your life and that you can create what you want to be, do, and have.

Unfortunately, we are continually being deflected from our certainty of purpose. People can and do interfere and destroy our certainty and, in turn, create a sense of defeat and frustration—*if we allow it*. For people may also support us in our goals and purpose.

To understand how we are deflected from our certainty of purpose, we might think of people as energy directors. Each of us directs the energy within us by the act of choice; but to choose wisely, we must be informed and aware that our energy flows may be crossed or opposed by other energy flows. As you look at the people you know, think of each as an energy director. The way they think and feel determines the way they direct their energy. For them to be healthy, happy, loving, and self-expressive, they must be aware, conscious, and responsible for the way they direct that powerful energy toward others and themselves.

Obviously, as our own energy directors, we have the same obligations. But we give other energy directors power over us, or other energy directors give us power over them. The consequence is that we spend much of our time and energy fighting and resisting other energy flows. And in the process, we are deflected from our certainty of purpose, if not from the purpose or goal itself.

I think of these energies as three basic flows: the helping flow, the crossing flow, and the opposing flow. The irony is that you do not have to stop and fight or resist other energy flows to achieve your purpose and be who you are. You can expand your own larger purpose in life to allow others to go where they are going and get what they want, just as you go where you are going and get what you want. Not to know this is a disaster to us all. To know that you *can* do this is freedom. You are a powerful creator, and every desire has the potential for fulfillment. And as an energy director, only you can *help*, *cross*, or *oppose* yourself in the attainment of your desires and purpose.

To illustrate what I mean, I recall an incident on the beach near my home. As I walked along one morning, I stopped to watch a small child about three years old. He was totally involved in a project. He'd fill his sand bucket with wet sand and then go to a level place and empty the bucket, carefully keeping the sand in the shape of the bucket. Back and forth he went, engrossed in this activity, until his grandmother approached him and made some suggestions of her own. The child was angry and frustrated. He was thrown off purpose before he had completed his task. However, as soon as his grandmother returned to her beach umbrella, he doggedly began filling the bucket with wet sand and emptying it just as before. His anger disappeared, and clearly he was happy again because he was once again pursuing his own purpose.

You can become like that little child at the beach. Regardless of what was yesterday or how you have handled relationships or how they have handled you, you can rehabilitate your certainty of self, purpose, and goals.

First, I want to share with you a personal experience in which I got off the track and lost my certainty. I'm a person who is usually happy, full of energy, supportive of others, and generally glad to be alive and who enjoys the game of life to the fullest. As I subsequently looked back over a period of six months, I had been gradually losing my aliveness, satisfaction, and certainty. It was such a gradual loss that I didn't notice it until I was on the verge of mental and physical collapse.

I use my body as my indicator to tell me what is going on in my mind: a change in mind and attitudes, a change in the body. I was tired and had difficulty sleeping much of the time. I discovered a sort of roller-coaster effect. I would be high, happy, and energetic one minute and bone-tired and despairing the next. There was turmoil in my job. There were people who appeared to be resisting me, and I had the feeling that I must push and shove to get me and my work going. I found days I didn't really want to go to work. I found the harder I tried, the worse I felt. I even thought perhaps I was in the wrong work and that the goals and purposes I had were no longer true for me. The clincher was the discovery that I wasn't having any fun in life.

I had to acknowledge that somehow I was off the track,

had lost my certainty of purpose, and that, for the sake of my very life, I had to get back on. Being in resistance to the flow of your natural self is Hell. Being in the flow of the spiritual life is Heaven, and I wanted to get back.

For a week I spent two or three hours each day writing out what appeared to be going on so that I could stand back and view my life. It wasn't easy at first. I was so confused that I found it hard to determine what I really wanted in my life. But I knew that, if I persisted day after day, the truth would eventually surface.

But even before I achieved clarity, I wrote out and said my affirmation: "I accept and know that whatever I need to know, be conscious of, and have cleared up in my life for me to be certain and happy and on purpose is revealed to me now. God is my source and all good is mine."

God always says "yes," but the creative force waits for us to speak our word. If you don't ask, you don't get. It's that simple.

Within a short time, things became clear to me. This clarity was triggered by a phone call from a friend who told how, during therapeutic hypnosis, she learned that she had given up her natural happy and loving self to gain the approval of her family. She had, in essence, killed off a part of herself to get back love.

I suddenly saw that I, too, had been gradually suppressing myself. I was trying to be what I thought my husband wanted, what my friends wanted, and what my congregation wanted. Ironically, all of this happened while I was receiving acclaim and prospering in my life. I discovered that deep within me I had a belief that I could have only so much success and so much happiness. I thought I was at the limit so I was sabotaging myself and my work through other people. I was doing whatever I could to get the approval of those who weren't approving, and I was killing myself. I didn't even see all those who absolutely loved and supported the real me. I only had eyes for rejection.

I was amazed because I thought I was beyond all that. Yet, it brought home to me how profoundly we are intertwined with others and how our beliefs control our actions, thoughts, and conditions. Actually, no one had truly suppressed me or killed my fun, aliveness, or desire for life: *I had done this.* I was the one who turned my life over to others and said: "Here, you be responsible for my loving myself and for my goal achievements, my prosperity, and all the rest!" I had made people my source and set myself up for disaster. *People are our avenue, not our source, of good.*

With this renewed consciousness, I felt as though the weight of the world had been lifted off me. I was free once again, and this renewed consciousness was like a revelation, a gift. For my life and power expanded to greater levels of certainty than ever before.

I was also aided by the new insight into how I had allowed other energy flows to suppress and deflect me. Other people are always there, and many of them are negative. But neither you nor I have to get caught up in their game. You see, we fear that, if we are true to ourselves, our purposes, and goals, we will be selfish and nonsupportive of others with their purposes and goals. This is untrue because the universe is set up as a win-win situation. When you are in harmony with life and love, you always win although you might not always get what you mistakenly think you ought to have. But you are always in your right place and so are others around you.

Suppressive people and organizations are not always immediately apparent. Nor are they necessarily committed to destroying the powers of others. It's just that they unconsciously think that's the only way they can be okay and have power. But if you don't play the suppression game, you'll transcend it and others will have to give it up as it affects you.

Most of us, unless totally clear on our connection with God and our infinite supply of good, will suppress others and ourselves to varying degrees. And when you are confronted with suppression from others, you will see something of yourself there. Don't let that worry you. Just be thankful for the awareness, and don't play the game.

There is really no need to fight negative energy flows. Step aside and allow them to flow past you. It is futile to try to change these negative energy directors. It merely encourages the craziness, and what you resist persists.

If nonresistance sounds strange, just remember that your happiness and love and acceptance come from yourself and God, not from others. Your place is not to judge, but to work on your own consciousness. Your outer world is a reflection or creation of your inner world. If there's confusion outside, clear up the confusion in your head and the outside will be cleared up.

There's nothing like the excitement of discovering that you can be totally yourself, achieve your goals, and live the way you choose. But this involves transformation or transcendence; and to transcend the ordinary level of life, you must understand the energy flows and how they affect you and others. You will recall that earlier I suggested that we view individuals as energy directors and that there were three kinds of energy flow. The first of these is the *helping* energy flow. All of us are certainly familiar with helping flows, even if we've never designated them as such. These are the flows from people telling you how to run your life. They are also the flows from people who have ideas and can assist you if you will allow them. Our tendency is to resist the helping flows.

Have you ever rejected a good idea someone gave you simply because you didn't think of it first? Or, have you ever done the very thing you didn't want to do, just to show the helpers you didn't want their advice? We've all played the game of resistance, and all it does is to deflect us from our purpose. The point is that some of the helping flows are beneficial and some are not. And you can choose. You don't have to sabotage your purpose by fighting and resisting parents, children, mates, friends, employers, and the like. Look to see if the advice or assistance is really good for you. If it is, say, "Yes, thank you," and give them the credit. If you don't think the advice or assistance will be good, say, "No, thank you," and do what you want to do yourself. The sad thing is that many, many people are off purpose, uncertain of themselves, and not getting any of life's goodies just because they don't want the would-be helpers to think that they were right.

The second energy flow that deflects us from our purpose is one that I call the *crossing* flow. And we're all familiar with this flow. This is the gossip, criticism, the negative energy that can knock us off balance and keep us there—if we let it. I know plenty of people who spend valuable time fighting criticism and trying to convince others that gossip isn't true. That's where their energy goes rather into achieving their purpose and reaching their goals. If you stop the pursuit of your purpose to deal with these things, your entire life will be spent and your energy, exhausted, in fighting little battles.

The irony is that those people aren't really trying to cross you or knock you off your purpose. It's just that their lives are not working because they don't know that they, too, are connected with an infinite source of abundance. Consequently, they may think you are taking their energy or keeping their lives from working. In retaliation, their crossing flow is involved with you or others who have doubt. If you buy into this crossing flow, you and they are tediously involved with the question of whether you can make it or not. What you do is give up your idea of who you are and accept another idea that is not true but is more widely held. Thus, mediocrity runs rampant on the planet. Transcend the flow to cross you, to criticize, to gossip, or to doubt you. Take a "so-what!" attitude. Remember that any idea you buy is yours, so why not choose what *you* want.

The third energy flow (a great deflector) is the *opposing* flow. "You can't do that and I won't let you." Sound familiar? Individuals directing opposing flows use all kinds of threats and fears to stop you. They may form a brick wall. But, as with a physical brick wall, there is a way around, over, or under. If you spend your energy trying to destroy the opposition, you can create much misery and sickness for yourself and others. Again, you must transcend—become bigger than—your opposition and see your goals as impregnably completed in your mind. And remember that, by using the law of creation, you will get there. This law, which bears repeating, is: Ideas will create the results in your life.

Certainty of purpose is knowing that you have the power within you to be, do, and have what you want in life. And it can be effortless, if you will ignore the would-be deflectors.

SELF-AWARENESS STRATEGIES
AND EXERCISES

■ OBSERVE

Notice those times when you know you are on purpose and those times when you know you are off purpose. Are you using others' resistance as your excuse for not following your own goals?

In what sorts of situations do you feel most suppressed? When do you feel depressed, slow, and unhappy? Which people do you feel light and happy with?

In what sort of situations do you feel most alive, creative, and talented? These are the areas of your natural talents and skills.

Watch your physical reactions to different situations. Notice when you are tired and when you are full of energy.

■ CHOOSE

Recognize now that you are responsible for whatever situation you find yourself in. When you are off purpose, say, "I am off purpose. I have allowed myself to lose sight of my goals." Accept the fact that you have allowed others to control you, or that you are trying to control someone other than yourself. If others distract you, say, "Okay, I choose to let others distract me."

Check to see what your payoff is for being off purpose or without purpose. Do you feel you "owe" it to others to let them distract you? Do you think if you pick a goal you will fail, or feel pressured to try to reach it? What are your *real* reasons for being off purpose?

▪ GIVE UP BLAME

Make whatever is going on with you at the moment okay. Don't blame yourself for being off purpose, just note that you are. Blaming others is a game; it's not the point. Give up the need for approval from others and be yourself.

It is equally pointless to make yourself wrong. Feeling guilty can be a great excuse for not getting on with life. Don't fall into that trap either.

List the beliefs you have about your purpose or lack of it. Do you think having goals will make you less flexible? Do you believe that successfully reaching your goals will make you less lovable?

Look at the judgments you are making about purpose and goals. Notice how these judgments set you up for making people, yourself included, right or wrong.

▪ CREATE IT THE WAY YOU WANT IT

List ten abilities that are natural and easy for you. Recall what your interests were when you were a child.

Let your mind soar and discover exactly the way you want to be. See yourself being certain of your purpose as you go through your daily affairs.

Ask yourself what you would do if money were no object and if you were free of any obligations to other people.

AFFIRMATIONS

1. I, _____, am a happy, healthy, intelligent person who enhances others by being real and true to myself.

2. It's perfectly right for me, _____, to want and to achieve my own unique purpose and goals.

3. As I, _____, live as I choose to, I am actually more loving and giving to my loved ones.

6

GOING BEYOND YOUR COMFORT ZONE

Risk is a necessary element in your self-development. It's absolutely necessary if you are to realize your God-given potential. In fact, your willingness to risk is a measure of your willingness to live life to its fullest. The dictionary defines risk as "the chance of injury, damage, or loss . . . the chance of the failure of your expectations." What the dictionary doesn't say is that, behind each of those chances, is the *opportunity* to learn and gain the fulfillment of your desires.

When you think of risk, you often feel threatened or fearful. Fear and risk seem to go together, like ham and eggs or peaches and cream. A sort of natural pairing, it would seem. Actually, as we shall see, risk can be a way of overcoming fear. The bottom line is: if you are going to have any fruitful activity in your life at all, you must be willing to risk.

We avoid risk for four reasons. First, we fear that we will get what we think we want, only to discover that we didn't want it all. Second, we fear failure and believe failure so painful we won't even try. Third, we fear we will lose what we already have. People spend a lot of energy trying to keep what they have and avoid what they fear. And fourth, we fear we will be successful and that we will not be able to handle our success.

A pernicious byproduct of fear is immobility. The phrase "frozen with fear" is usually associated with a traumatic event like war, physical assault, or accident, but such immobility can be an ingredient in our daily lives. We become frozen mentally and physically when we think of taking action to change our lives. There is a part of us that wants to keep things just the way they are, no matter how unhappy we are with them. To cling to the familiar, we will pay almost any price.

An extreme example is the story my great-grandmother used to tell of a woman whose husband beat her regularly. When asked why she didn't leave the man, the woman replied: "I can't leave. I don't know what I would do out there." This woman was unwilling to risk going "out there" for fear that it would be worse than where she was.

To one degree or another, we all do this, over and over again. No matter how painful the familiar, we put up with it because we fear the new. We call this unwillingness to risk "security."

To transcend fear, you must be willing to risk. You must be willing to go beyond your comfort zone. While comfort zones differ among us, the comfort zone is essentially the level of our past experiences. It falls somewhere between the lowest and the highest good you can accept for yourself. We are all familiar with the convict who, after years of imprisonment, is finally confronted with freedom and doesn't want to leave the security of the prison walls. In a way, we are all like the prisoner. We remain in the familiar situation, even when it falls short of happiness and fulfillment, because we are afraid to expand our comfort zone.

We forget that life is to be *lived*. Life is about full self-expression and self-fulfillment. To live fully, you must expand and grow, and that requires risk. When we settle for the familiar, for safety, it's because we've forgotten that God is our only security. Growth and change can be exciting when we depend on the source rather than on our mates, our friends, our government—on people, places, and things.

There is no lasting security in the physical or material world: people change, money devaluates, governments collapse, companies retrench and fail. Nothing is constant in the physical world. Our quest for security in the physical world is doomed because the world is designed for change.

The only constant is God and the spiritual world. When you realize that God is constant and that you are an individualized expression of God, you can create what you want regardless of what's going on around you. You are free to risk, to give up what's comfortable and familiar in favor of that which is satisfying, fulfilling, and exciting.

Some people are willing to settle for dull, boring, drab, and unfulfilling jobs in the name of security. Others are adventurers who welcome the challenge and excitement of risk. Many of my management seminars are conducted for people who work totally on commission. They have no regular salary, no pension plans, no unions. If they don't produce, they have no income and soon, no job. Yet they love their work. They accept the excitement of challenge. They are willing to risk, and many have been richly rewarded for their risk.

On the other hand, look at the ones who spend a lifetime working for the government because it offers security. Those who are there because of the benefits, the job security, lack aliveness. I have a girlfriend who works in a veterans' hospital. She hates her job but won't leave it because of the benefits and job security. She's a lovely, talented woman; but we don't spend much time together anymore because I've gotten tired of her complaints, and she finds my willingness to take risks uncomfortable.

As Henry David Thoreau wrote in *Walden*, "The mass of men lead lives of quiet desperation." This describes a tragically large number of people. These are the people who have given up on life. Immobilized by fear, they are suffering death in small doses. Each one fails to recognize that *action cures fear.*

You must be willing to confront your fears and go through them or they will continue to run your life. I can remember when I was terrified of public speaking. Even in school I was afraid to raise my hand or speak in class. Yet today I earn the major part of my income speaking to large crowds. What's more, I enjoy it!

Looking back I realize I was afraid people would criticize me and tell me my ideas were no good. I was afraid I was going to lose. But I survived and learned an invaluable lesson: a good way to handle this fear, or any other, is to do so in small increments or small doses. First, I tried speaking to small, familiar groups; and in the beginning my body literally shook with fear. But I survived and kept speaking, gradually to larger groups. And gradually I learned to enjoy the excitement and, as a result, my speaking improved. I even learned I could survive the loss of approval when I spoke poorly. To learn *that* was exciting in itself.

When we think we have lost or failed, we tend to exaggerate the experience. If we're honest, we realize that we don't fail all of the time and that, in most of those failures, there are positive lessons for growth. Clearly, there are more people who have accepted us than have rejected us. Yet, we take those few rejections, allow ourselves to be immobilized by fear, and resolve never to get in such a position again.

We take the loss of a job as a signal to find job security rather than to look for a job where we can express ourselves and thereby succeed. We lose an investment and use that as an excuse not to invest rather than as a lesson about how to invest wisely.

I know a man who lived a high-risk style of life. Through his risks, he created a huge financial institution. A company with a heavy investment in his enterprise went bankrupt and set in motion a domino effect, which eventually brought down this man's own business. He lost virtually everything. Now he lives his life very conservatively, risk free. But he doesn't have very much either. He's afraid to risk again. His belief system informs him that he risked once and lost and that never again can he face the disillusionment of the collapse of his dreams. His attitude is to live with what he has, devoted to the old concept that a bird in the hand is worth two in the bush. A lot of us believe that. Only thing wrong with that concept is that not even *that* is safe because circumstances are always changing.

Of course, many people who have earned large fortunes tell how they first went broke—and often more than once. But they dared to risk again. They listened to their true selves and went on to win. Those opting for safety negated their inner selves, and most are bitter and blame others or the world for doing them in. They don't seem to realize that they still have the power within themselves to create exactly what they want, if they will only risk it.

Risk is exciting; but more than that, risk stimulates aliveness in the person taking the chance. Through risk, we have the opportunity to experience the kind of success that develops our certainty of how the universe works. By experiencing, going through your fears, you can learn that you master the world. Avoid risk and be run by fear, and you allow the world—the environment and other people—to control you.

The willingness to take risk simply means you are willing to go out beyond your familiar niche. There is a first time for everything, and we often feel the sense of risk (and fear) on those occasions. When you first tried walking, you fell. But you were close enough to your higher self to know that walking would expand your life. So you were willing to risk falling until you got it right. Then, as with all new things, you succeeded. Walking worked, and you were comfortable with what had been a scary situation.

So, figure out exactly what you want. This is necessary so that you will recognize it when it comes along. And when it does, as it will, you must be willing to go for it. Be willing to risk. Know that action overcomes fear and that you can go for your goal in small steps.

SELF-AWARENESS STRATEGIES AND EXERCISES

▣ OBSERVE

Notice those times when you are willing to take a risk. How do you feel? What's involved in the risk? What do you think you will gain? What do you think you will lose?

How do you feel about others who take risks? Do you support them or do you discourage them? Why?

Notice those times when you are unwilling to risk. What are you afraid you will lose? Do you avoid challenges because of fear? Are you afraid to ask for what you want? Do you think people will leave you? What are you *really* afraid of? Why?

■ CHOOSE
Accept yourself the way you are. If you are unwilling to take risks with people, say, "I choose not to risk with people." If you feel fear, say: "I choose to feel afraid." "I choose to not expand." "I choose to hide or be safe." Remember, you are responsible for your own life. Take responsibility for your feelings and actions about risk.

■ GIVE UP BLAME
You don't need to feel guilty if you are unwilling to take risk now. You are in the process of changing your life, and it won't help if you make yourself wrong. Learn to risk in small steps.

Others are *not* the reason you are unwilling to risk. If you are afraid that someone will leave you, that's your fear. And if they leave you, then let them go. When you blame others, you are giving up your power.

■ CREATE IT THE WAY YOU WANT IT
Take a look at the way you want to be, the way you want to feel about risk. Visualize situations in your past where you wish you had taken a risk. What would you have

done? What would you have said? How would you have felt if you had taken that risk? What would the result have been?

Picture risk situations that you think may come up in the future. What is the result you want? Imagine asking for and getting that result. What will you say? What will you do? Think about how you will feel when you get the result you want. See yourself already having achieved your goal. Write a specific affirmation that says exactly how you want to respond in risky situations. Read it aloud at least twice a day.

AFFIRMATIONS

1. I, _____, am willing and able to expand my comfort zone effortlessly.

2. I, _____, ask for what I want, tell the truth, and accept my own self-worth with all people in all situations with positive results for all.

3. I, _____, have the talent, time, opportunity, and willingness I need to accomplish all my goals and objectives.

7

GOOD HEALTH IS YOUR NATURAL STATE

For the majority of the people on this planet, good health is a natural state of well-being. But with all of our preoccupation with illness, the incessant visits to the doctor, the continual pill taking, you'd never know that good health is a natural state.

Most people, in fact, go to the doctor to find out if they are healthy. We rely on authorities outside ourselves to tell us the condition of our own beingness. We put doctors in the position of being gods rather than recognizing that each of us is *the* authority for the condition of his or her own body. Our bodies are our own, personal responsibility.

You are, first, a spiritual being, and health is natural for you. You have to get in the way of your own nature to create sickness. Your body is a response system that takes its signals from you. When your mind, your belief system, is in harmony with who you are spiritually and you realize God is your source, you have to go out of your way to impose illness upon yourself.

My own experience leads me to believe that sickness is always a problem-solving device, but a *faulty* one. It's a device we use when we want to avoid confrontation with unpleasant reality. This is acknowledged both by physicians who practice psychosomatic medicine and by those in the psychological and psychiatric therapies as well.

Most of us live with varying degrees of stress in our lives. Stress is a response we suffer when we are not comfortable in our various relationships and feel threatened. Medical researchers are beginning to discover that there seems to be a causal relationship between stress and visible physical ailments, such as cancer, arthritis, heart disease, and various stomach ailments. There is also evidence that many of these ailments are often preceded by emotional trauma.

Both stress and emotional trauma are the results of a separation from God as the source, which, in essence, is separation from the knowledge that you have the power to create and control your own life, that you are able to say "yes" when you want to and "no" when you want to.

Look at those times when you feel really alive. Usually it's a day when you don't feel any pressure or obligations, when you are among fun-loving people and don't feel threatened in any way. Or it can be a day when you are alone, doing something you enjoy. In any event, it's a day when you just tingle with aliveness.

Unhappily, such days are too rare for many of us. We experience them only so long as we are away from home, school, our job, or any environment where we feel a suppressive influence. Notice how your body feels when you're full of joy. Contrast this feeling with what your body has when you're down and depressed. Your body is trying to tell you something.

Many people are simply not conscious of their bodies until they get sick. I find that, when I truly trust my body, it will tell me what's going on and what's right for me. A simple experiment is to listen to your body when you are deciding what to eat. As you tune in to yourself, your body will say "yes" or "no" to certain items on the menu.

You see, the body is a wonderful feedback machine. If you listen you will discover that it talks to you. When you get a headache, your body is trying to tell you something, usually about the tension and stress you are feeling. All of your aches and pains, mild and severe, are your body's method of communicating with you.

I have a friend who is a writer, and she tells me that, at times, she gets arthritis in her thumb so bad she literally cannot pick up a pencil or use her hand to type. She has discovered that this is her body's way of telling her that she has hidden angry and resentful feelings from herself. She knows that the pain is a signal to get honest and find out what's going on and that, as soon as she admits to the anger and lets it go, the pain goes away. The key is to be willing to listen to your body and deal with what's going on.

The hard-to-accept fact is that health is a byproduct of your mental and spiritual attitude. It can be a *well* byproduct or an *ill* byproduct. You, and only you, can make the choice.

The one thing we cannot get away from is our own power to create. We're always creating; and if we do it unconsciously, we usually create trouble. On the other hand, if we create consciously, with the willingness and courage to be healthy, to make our own decisions, and to be self-reliant, if we have the courage to be constructively selfish, we ultimately give good service to ourselves and to others.

When we lack the courage to take care of ourselves, we

unconsciously try to solve problems by becoming sick, which is probably the poorest way to handle a situation. Illness is, of course, an alarm system. It's the final means the body has of notifying you that you are doing something wrong. If you observe the circumstances when the alarm is first sounded, you can often take care of the situation before the illness becomes severe. The sickness alarm usually occurs when we are in a situation where we feel threatened, when we think we can lose. You ignore such warnings at your own risk.

Accidents are another warning that we often ignore. We literally can beat ourselves up when we're judging ourselves or others, are fearful, are feeling guilt or anger. Next time you stub your toe or hit your thumb with a hammer, stop and ask yourself what you were really feeling just before the "accident." People can actually cause heart attacks, cancer, and other serious diseases because they are not willing to become conscious and deal with their true feelings.

Dr. Don Dill, a respected medical doctor in the San Diego area, tells me that he is able to trace a pattern of accidents and illness in his patients. He says that, if a person doesn't handle the minor pain, such as a headache or hitting a finger with a hammer, that pain can be the starting point of a more serious condition, one that may occur even years later. It's almost as if we feel guilty on some intuitive level if we don't respond to the body's pain message, and we continue to create more pain and sickness until we can no longer ignore it.

You must become conscious of the fact that no one can threaten you unless you buy into that threat. Your body lets you know when you are buying into such a situation. You see, your body wants to be healthy. That's why it doesn't lie to you. It's people who lie, and lying is such an accepted way of life on this planet that telling the truth requires great courage.

Sickness is a means of avoiding confrontation, of avoiding telling the truth. We are afraid that, if we tell the truth, people will know who we are and will know that we are not all we pretend to be. We'd rather put on our act and lie than tell the truth and be healthy. But our bodies don't lie.

You have only to look at people's bodies to see how much they love or hate themselves and how much they deceive themselves. Getting sick is a means of self-punishment for many. There are others who think of disease as a way to gain comfort. They actually think they will be safer sick than healthy.

Look at the suave, sophisticated businessman driving his big car, yet his stomach is eaten with ulcers. Or the young woman executive smartly dressed and on her way up the corporate ladder and who is plagued with migraines. Or the housewife surrounded by labor-saving machines who is too tired to spend time with her husband or children. Or the man who drinks to excess and suffers hangovers several times a week. Each of these people is hiding from the truth their bodies are telling them. They are ignoring the symptoms of fear. They have lost the knowledge that they are responsible for their bodies and that, through conscious awareness, they can change their belief systems and create the vibrant, good health they want.

While there is presently a movement toward the development of holistic medicine, we are rarely taught that we can be healthy. Just think of the atmosphere we create to convince people that illness is natural. Listen to the people around you, and notice what media advertisements are saying: "It's the flu season. Get your aspirin and stay out of the cold." "It's the cold season. Get the antiseptic mouthwash." "It's your menstrual period. Get something for cramps." "You're getting old. Take minerals and vitamins. Get ready to lose your teeth, your hearing, your sight." And on and on.

Did you ever notice that not everyone who gets wet and cold gets the flu? Or that some women don't have cramps? And that others in seemingly stressful situations don't get headaches? How many elderly have excellent eyesight, their original teeth, and good hearing? Such people are not just lucky: they are in touch with their natural good health.

Obviously, we all have a responsibility for the good care of our bodies, but this is not so much a matter of medicine as of avoiding excesses in what we eat and drink, using common nutritional sense, providing our bodies with needed physical exercise, and raising our consciousness to recognize that good health is natural. Instead, most of us act as though we believe sickness is inevitable. The only solution we can see is to have enough medication to ease the pain. As I mentioned, the holistic medicine groups are in the process of developing ways to support our natural well-being, but presently members of the medical profession are set up for crisis and emergency situations. If you don't require surgery or have an incurable disease, they are often not sure what to do.

Given the belief systems most of us have, the truth just doesn't fit the way we see life. Most people think the body creates the disease and then you have to handle the illness. This puts the cart before the horse. Such people refuse to see that we mentally create what's going on in our bodies. They think there's some power out there in the universe that's directing all the illness.

Look how much power we give the germ. We think this tiny, microscopic thing is going to determine the destiny of the human body. We give more power to that tiny life particle than we do to the human being who is born in tune with, and is one with, the universe and God, the same God who is the ultimate creator of all, even the germ.

Of course, there are germs, but scientists and doctors have verified that each of us has a physical immune system and that we get sick when there is a breakdown in this system. Again, our bodies are the alarm system that tells us when the natural protective process is not working. And it is our consciousness that controls the system.

How do you reach the consciousness that assures good health? Accept that you began life healthy and that health is natural. Ask yourself: "What have I done in life? What are my attitudes? What are the situations that ultimately created disease or the lack of body harmony and unity?" Look back at the times you were ill and examine the correlations with your emotional state at the time. What kind of changes were going on in your life, and how did you react to these changes?

Psychological studies confirm that change is a crisis time for most of us. But change is constant and eternal, even though we resist it. We fight it because we want to hang on to our relationships, cling to our possessions, our children, our money. We fight change because we think sameness is the avenue to security and stability. That obviously is not so. Our principal achievement when we resist change is to put stress on our bodies and, thereby, to create illness.

It's this fact that allows spiritual healings. When Jesus healed the sick, he first forgave them, which set the stage for their recovery through their total acceptance of their physical and spiritual selves. These seemingly miraculous healings are not really miracles: they are simply an example of what can happen when a person becomes aligned with the truth. It's unfortunate that we experience so little of this, but it's there, ready for us to use at any time.

Sickness is a form of dying, or, if you will, a form of killing, whether it's killing cells in your own body or simply killing a good time. This kind of dying occurs because you have mentally and spiritually separated yourself from God the source. If you accept that you and God are one, you can have what you want in life, including good health. You don't let your fears of change make you ill because you accept that you always have to let go of the old to have the new. You accept that, inevitably, when you make your security dependent on a person, place, or thing, you set yourself up for crisis, stress—and illness.

We must be willing to live and be well. We must know that God is the source, not others, and we must give up our positions of right and wrong. As we become willing to communicate with others, we enhance our willingness to have good health and to participate and grow.

What I have said above applies to the tremendous majority of the people born. There are exceptions, and I am often asked about these. What, I am asked, about the child born with a birth or genetic defect? These conditions can be mild or severe and can affect in varying degrees the physical body, the brain, or both. Sometimes these conditions lead to an early death; but more often, the severely handicapped child lives a relatively long life. Usually the question is put to me this way: "How can a loving God allow such a painful condition to exist?" When phrased that way, the question puts God outside and in fact denies the omnipresence of the Spirit.

A more enlightened way to put the question is this: "How do these tragic happenings fit in with the idea that we can create the life we want? Who would choose such a condition?" I must acknowledge that I don't have the complete answer, but I do know that Jesus, through consciousness and right relationship with God, was able to raise the dead, restore sight to the blind, and cause the crippled to walk. The essence of each of us—including the afflicted—is that Consciousness, that Spirit, that God within. In the case of a child, this explanation is particularly difficult to accept because we think of children as helpless, dependent, and incapable of knowing enough to make the right choice. But we are falling into judgment of God when we think one form is right and another is wrong. We are confronted with a condition that exists, and we don't know why God allows it to exist.

Nothing is gained in such situations by torturing ourselves with the resentful whys: we only make ourselves sick. For such situations, I can only suggest that your life will work better and you will be of true service to the one so afflicted if you recognize the Spirit within and accept the challenge to love and see through to the essence of the person involved. Most of us know some family that has handled this problem that way, and we are profoundly moved by the almost tangible aura of God's love that surrounds such people.

SELF-AWARENESS STRATEGIES
AND EXERCISES

■ OBSERVE

Notice those times when you feel alive and healthy. What are you doing? Whom are you with?

Notice when you start to feel sick. What's been going on in your life? What problems have you had recently? What sort of tension have you been experiencing?

Notice how you feel around people who are healthy. Don't you tend to feel better?

Now watch what happens when you are around someone who is sick. What happens to you? Do you tend to plug in?

■ CHOOSE

Whatever your health situation is at the moment, take personal responsibility for it. If you're sick, say, "I have chosen to be ill at this time." Now, find what sort of problem you are solving with this illness. Are you avoiding something? Say, "I am using sickness to avoid this." Are you sick to get attention? Accept that, up until now, sickness has been your way of feeling loved. Be honest with yourself, and accept yourself just the way you are.

■ GIVE UP BLAME

When we find that we have created illness in ourselves, we tend to make ourselves wrong, which only makes the situation worse. Don't blame yourself. Just accept that you are responsible and know that you don't have to stay sick.

It's also easy to blame outside forces—the weather, drafts, the food we ate, and so on.

■ CREATE IT THE WAY YOU WANT IT

Visualize yourself free from sickness. Imagine what your life would be like if you experienced vibrant good health. Where would you go? What would you do? Create a clear mental picture of your healthy, alive self. If someone asks you how you are, tell them you feel fine. Don't complain about your health. Don't plug into the warnings about colds and flu.

Write an affirmation that states exactly the way you want to feel. Read it aloud at least twice a day.

AFFIRMATIONS

1. I, _____, know that good health is my natural state.

2. I, _____, knowing that God is my source, feel healthy and alive.

3. I, _____, have abundant strength and energy to do exactly what I want.

8

DEATH IS A LIVING EXPERIENCE

The beliefs we hold about death have tremendous influence on the quality of our lives. The fears we have of our own deaths, the fears we have that our loved ones will die—these fears compel us to consume our energies trying to avoid death. We waste our precious energies trying to avoid loss when these energies should be applied to living. To live freely, we must be able to handle death, and our ability to handle it depends upon the beliefs we hold about it.

Most of us perceive death as a finality, the end of everything. Actually, death is the name we give to the end of a form. It's the completion of a cycle, but it's not a finality. In that sense, there is no death in the universe. Everywhere in the universe we see the completion of cycles.

Take a match, light it, and watch it burn until the match and the flame are gone. Only the smoke remains. Well, we think, the match is over. It died. Actually, the smoke is carbon, a basic element in life, and goes back into the carbon chain. A tree dies and decays into dust. And from its dust emerge new forms of life. In this cyclic sense, the embryo dies to become an infant, the infant dies to become a child, the child dies to become an adolescent, the adolescent dies to become an adult, and eventually the adult dies. To become what?

Before I attempt to answer that question, I wish to emphasize that, in the physical world, no form endures forever. All forms proceed through various cycles of completion and regeneration. But in the spiritual world, the essence of our being is everlasting. What form this everlasting essence takes following physical death is a matter of tremendous speculation among theologians. Whether the physical form is reincarnated, as some believe, or assumes a new role in a celestial kingdom, as others believe, we do not know in a provable sense. I am confident in my faith that the essence of our being is everlasting, but I am also humble enough to acknowledge that I don't know what succeeding form this essence might take.

The most important thing, it seems to me, is to examine the attitudes about death that are compelling in the influence they have on our lives. If we observe these attitudes objectively, we will learn to have more life in our years, more aliveness in each moment, and we won't live our lives in preparation for death as many people do. You know the expression "the day you are born, you begin to die." It suggests that, for some people, preparation for death begins very early. Preparation for death picks up in the middle years. I recall that, when my great-grandmother reached seventy-five, she would buy no more new clothes. And if someone gave her a new dress, she responded: "Don't waste your money on me. I'm going to be dead, anyway." Think how much more sensible it would have been had she thought: "Even if I get a new dress the day I die, so what. Look at the joy and pleasure it gives me."

Life is to be lived moment to moment, not in preparation for death, but in preparation for more life. I knew a wonderful man who, though elderly and suffering from terminal cancer, was learning Spanish while in the hospital. He was taking these Spanish lessons so that he could communicate with the Mexican help in his home in Palm Springs. And, yes, he did die. Now most people would say: "All that money and effort spent on Spanish were wasted. He never got to use it."

But you can't waste that kind of effort. If he got one moment of enjoyment or any sense of achievement from his effort, that alone provided value. And I'm convinced that what you gain in this life is never wasted because you take it with you to your next expression. Wherever you go, in whatever form, you take who you are with you.

We all hold beliefs about how old a person should be when he or she dies, and feel that there is some age when death is appropriate. What about those people in Russia who live to be 135 or older and are still physically fit? In our country, we are afraid of old age, and this fear itself hastens the arrival of death. Again, I emphasize, we should be living for the sake of living, not in preparation for death.

Then, there is the old and widely held belief that life here and now is for suffering, that we must live through this "veil of tears" to prepare for the next step: Heaven. We must live a life of suffering to pay the price for something good that's going to happen when we die. That's nonsense! The Kingdom of Heaven is right now, and Heaven is a state of mind. Right now there are people on this planet living in Hell; others are living in Heaven. Both groups have made their choices, consciously or unconsciously.

It is critically important for you to look at your beliefs about death, your beliefs about old age, your beliefs about

sickness, and your belief about how many years you are supposed to live. I often hear people say: "Well, I don't want to
live too long, because I am destined to live fast." We can look
among certain movie stars, those the publicists called "sex
symbols," and observe "untimely" deaths among these young
and beautiful women. When one's whole life is based on being gorgeous now, it is easy for the fear of old age and the loss
of attention to foster unconscious beliefs that become a setup
for death. From such a situation, we get the suicides, the accidental and "untimely" deaths.

The point I'm trying to make is that the way you handle
your life is the major factor in the way you die. Earlier, in
discussing health, I pointed out that sickness is faulty problem
solving by persons out of harmony with themselves. The same
principle is involved in much of dying. Consciously or unconsciously, a person says: "I have a problem, and I think the way
I'll handle it is to choose the option of death." Variations on
this theme are: "I'm tired of this reality"; "I'm bored"; "My
purpose is over"; "I've lived fully here, and I want to see
what's at the next level." Whatever the apparent causes of
death, the real cause comes from the deceased and may be the
result of being afraid of this life and not knowing how to
handle it, of wanting to get even with someone, of wanting to
make others pay the price for not being nice, of being in over
your head—I can go on and on. The need or desire for death
comes out of the person, and the circumstances that will lead
to the transition, or death, are set in motion by these prior
conditions.

Just as *life* is the product of the being and not of the body,
so death is caused by the *being*, not the body. Just as God is
the creator of the universe, each one of us is a creator of our
lives. So, as the causes of death come out of us, there is ap-

parent ambiguity: in one sense, we are ready to go on to the next level of being; in another sense, we are afraid of handling this level. That's why I say, "Death is a living experience." What I wish to focus attention on is that we can handle this level of being and can live life more fully, more easily, more joyfully, if we live to *live*, not live to avoid dying or to prepare for death, if we accept that we don't need to have our happiness at some other time: we need to have it now!

When I said earlier that the essence of you does not die, I was not trying to avoid the apparency of what we call death. One day there is life in the physical form; the next day there is no life in that form. So, we say the form has died and then the body decays. The apparency is that everybody dies physically, but I am certain the essence does not die.

Whether reincarnation is true or not, it is true that, physiologically speaking, each of us is the culmination of life to this date. You are the end product of all life before you. It is historically clear that we are constantly expanding in our intelligence. Obviously, the Neanderthal man was not who we are. But the Neanderthal man played a part in who we have become. And, in the same way, we will be a part of the sum of later life.

Consider also that your body is composed of the elements that have been on this planet forever, the same elements that will compose the physical forms of the future. Clearly, even at the physical level, we are all part of a continuum in which one form fades away for another to take its place. So, even in the physical sense, it is hard to make the argument that we die.

As for the spiritual level of our being, the teachings of Jesus about immortality make it clear that we live forever. For example, through my spiritual awareness, I have a sense within myself that I have never been born and that I shall never die.

I know I am *here* this time to participate in life, to expand, to grow, to share, to express, to be.

Philosophers search for the meaning of life with mixed results, and there are individuals who kill themselves when they can't find it. Perhaps, the meaning of life, like the purloined letter, is so obvious that we have overlooked it. Could it be that the meaning is just *to be*? I look out my window at the ocean, at its beauty and its mystery. What's its purpose? What's its meaning? Despite the fact that each wave is a gift of beauty, there's nothing to suggest that the ocean is there for any reason other than just to be. Spiritually speaking, that's our purpose: *to be*.

And spiritually speaking, I have always been and shall always be: the very essence of me is always there. This spiritual law is comparable to the physical law concerning the conservation of energy. This law states that, in any closed or isolated system, the total amount of energy is constant. Thus, within the system, energy is never lost: it simply changes form. Likewise spirit, or essence, is never lost: it simply changes form.

Throughout the universe, everything is made up of the same basic elements. In the physical world, form is a visible expression of molecular structure, of the way in which these elements are combined. The infinite variety of forms we see and enjoy about us results from various combinations and permutations of these basic elements within molecular structures. In the change of form, there is no absolute loss of substance, of essence.

So, it's perfectly consonant with the laws of the universe that I have always existed and shall always exist. And this is taught in the various religions: Hinduism, Buddhism, Judaism, and Christianity. I am one with God. I am one with the source. Whatever my form, I continue to exist, to be.

The enlightened ones have always asked the question: "Who am I?" Each of us may expand our consciousness by asking of ourselves: "Who am I?" You may ask: "Am I my body?" "Am I my job?" "Am I my relationships, my possessions?" "Am I my point of view?" "Am I my thoughts, my religion?" You may extend this list of questions, and you will find that you are not any of these things. For all of them constantly change, but you remain. There is something still there, something that has always been there. So, to know who we are, we have to know who we are not.

As I indicated earlier, through our failures to handle our living in a positive way, we choose the ways we die. We create fatal health conditions, the faulty solutions to problems in living. We have accidents and suicides. From my point of view, all deaths, consciously or unconsciously, are suicides. In the universe there are only law and order, no accidents. And so it is with death. The circumstances of accidents may be very, very complex; but I am convinced that a profound analysis of the victims of accidents would show that somewhere previously, consciously or unconsciously, they made a choice for an escape from the problems of living.

All of which inevitably brings us back to the problems we encounter in living. Most of us live our lives out of ignorance, not out of the enlightenment that reveals our prime options. Functioning from the Spirit, you recognize that you have unlimited opportunity, unlimited options to handle your life in a very positive way.

In my counseling, I frequently encounter people who are contemplating suicide. The irony is that they don't actually want death; instead, they want more life, but don't know how to get it. They want happiness, health and love, self-expression and abundance. They want to live, but they don't know how.

In effect, they say: "The only way to be free of an existence that is killing me is to die." So, they get the very thing they don't want: death.

In titling this chapter "Death Is a Living Experience," I wanted to point out, among other things, how fears concerning our own death and the deaths of those we love unnecessarily preoccupy so much of our daily living. We should not seek death, but neither should we fear it.

Earlier I referred to the fact that, rather than treating death as a *finality*, we should treat it as the *completion* of a phase or form. The essential tragedy is that so many of us die so far short of the *completion* of our lives. And by *completion*, I mean the realization of that divine creative potential with which we are all born. Similarly, the saddest aspect of the loss of a loved one is the possibility that our relationship with that one was *uncompleted*. What I'm saying is that each of us, through enlightenment, has the obligation and opportunity to live a *completed* life. It is inevitable that each of us must physically die someday, but that occasion can be an *appropriate* occasion if we develop and concentrate our consciousness on *living*, on realizing our divine potential. Do that and death takes care of itself.

As for the death experience itself, there is accumulated evidence that it is not a fearful experience but a joyful one. Dr. Elisabeth Kübler-Ross has conducted years of research with people who died medically—in an accident, on the operating table, by drowning—but were subsequently revived, brought back to life. In her interviews with these people, Dr. Kübler-Ross found that they all had experienced transcendent happiness. They had moved into a new level of consciousness outside their bodies and had found it to be a joyous experience.

Sean Hall, a young boy afflicted with leukemia, had just such an experience. Shortly before he died, he lapsed into a deathlike coma but after a time, regained consciousness. Totally coherent, he told his mother, Darlene: "I've just experienced God. God loves me and I am a wonderful boy. Mother, I'm fine. I am happy. I am going where I want to go, and it's beautiful." And then he died.

I have come across a number of other people who have shared with me their experiences during such brief crossovers into the hereafter. These are responsible people, not "kooks." The point of it all is that, as the door closes to this life, another door opens, and *there is something there.*

Clearly, death is not something to be feared. But I emphasize that it is not something to be looked forward to, either. Life is for living now, moment to moment, to extract all that it can give us. And when we die, we will be living at another level, moment to moment.

But we do need to know how to handle our own deaths and the deaths of others. I find in my ministry that people are afraid of others who are dying, that they are even afraid of the family members who are close to those who are dying. And in the funerals I conduct, I find that people want to do or say something to the loved ones left behind, but don't know what to do or say. Similarly, when I go to hospitals where someone is dying, others around them don't know what to say or do.

Thus, those who are dying often find that they are isolated and have no one with whom to share their feelings. Friends and family members who formerly were close seem alienated. They are so afraid of death that they won't even allow the dying person to experience death. I know, personally, that I want to experience my death and to be conscious of it. I want to experience it just as I experienced birth, a sunny day, or an accomplishment.

For those who die before we do, we must try to project how we would wish to be treated under the same circumstances. I know I want people to love me and treat me as I am treated in life now. If I have someone I have to meet, I am the only one who can handle it. But I want love and support. I want to share and communicate, because sharing and communication are what life's about. I don't want others to be afraid of me because I'm dying. I want them to touch me, to laugh with me, to cry with me. I want them to know me, and I want to know that their lives have been enhanced by my presence. I want to know that I have made a difference. And I don't want them to suffer guilt: I want to be remembered with joy.

In the aftermath of the death of a loved one, we experience grief, anger, and resentment. What grips us is the knowledge of uncompleted relationships. But to say "good-bye" to a relationship, you must first have said "hello." You must have loved that other person, released him, allowed him to be who he was and who he was not.

Unfortunately, most of us have dangling relationships. So, when someone is dying, it is really an opportunity for us and we'd better take it. We have the opportunity to complete the relationship. And when we have completed the relationship, death will leave us with little grief because we will have no guilt.

Our misunderstanding of love is such that we think that, if we don't grieve, we didn't love. Or that, if we come to love someone else, we are not showing proper respect for the dead. But if we look at God as the source, we realize that you and I and all the others share the same essence. It doesn't matter how many people I love. To really fail the departed one is to fail to love again.

When I conduct a funeral, I say: "If our friend or loved one were with us now, what would she say to us, now that she is on a level to view this life objectively? She would say, 'Are you really *living* now moment to moment?'" Because the next step is still moment to moment. In the absolute, there is no time or space, so there is no birth, no death. There is no past, no future. Everything is now.

I've heard it said that, if we all knew we had only a half hour of existence left on this planet, the phone lines would be clogged and the highways congested by people, all trying to say, "I love you." That's the bottom line. That's what's left. To live and to love, we must understand what death is— spiritually, mentally, and physically. We must live life freely, in fear neither of what we don't have nor of what we could lose. We must live for what we do have and for what we can experience. We must live life moment to moment, savoring fully each of these precious increments.

SELF-AWARENESS STRATEGIES AND EXERCISES

■ OBSERVE

Have you had someone close to you die? Notice how you felt. Were you angry, frustrated, afraid, or lonesome?

How do you feel when you hear about death? How do you feel when you think of your own death? Do you feel fear? Do you feel resentment?

Get in touch with all of your reactions to death: death in general, the death of those close to you, and your own death.

■ CHOOSE
Remember that you are in control of your own emotions and feelings. If you have experienced anger, frustration, and fear about the death of a loved one, accept those feelings. If you feel negative emotions when you think about your own death, accept those emotions. You can choose how you feel, but first you must accept yourself and love yourself just the way you are.

■ GIVE UP BLAME
Negative emotions are common when one is confronted with death, and often they are the result of suppressed anger. Our minds often subconsciously say: "How could that person have left me?" Or, "How could God have done such a thing?" Know that we don't have all the answers to these questions, but you will only destroy yourself if you blame. Remember not to blame yourself for whatever it is that you feel.

■ CREATE IT THE WAY YOU WANT IT
Visualize how you would like to feel about the subject of death. See how you would like to behave at a funeral. Picture yourself experiencing these things. Continue until you have come to terms with the idea of death, knowing that it is, indeed, part of the process of life.

AFFIRMATIONS

1. I, _____, accept that I don't have all of the answers about death and that I'm comfortable with that.

2. I, _____, always know just how to respond when another loses a loved one.

3. I, _____, am responsible for my feelings and can control and put to constructive use all of my emotions, including those about death.

9

FOOD AND OTHER FAULTY SUBSTITUTES

Our body is the vehicle through which we express ourselves, and the appearance and the health of the body are reflections of the ideas we hold. In the sense that we are all spirit expressing form, each one of us is complete and perfect—with or without fat or, for that matter, with or without a body. As Einstein taught us, mass and energy are differentiated principally by form. Your body is a form of energy slowed down to assume the appearance of mass. And the mind directs the energy that determines the form. You do have the power to create the form you desire to live in.

Don't forget that your body, as well as everything physical in life, is an effect of a prior cause. The cause is in your mind where you direct the energy flow. The beliefs and attitudes you hold about yourself and your life are manifest in your body.

The first point to keep firmly in mind is that you are complete and perfect regardless of what your body looks like. In fact, there is within every heavy body a slender body. You may choose to change your form by losing weight, but first you must know that you don't have to be slender to be accept-able to others. While it is true that fat people can create neg-ative reactions—even hostility—in others, the important point, as this entire book emphasizes, is not how others view you but *how you view yourself.* If you are truly comfortable with your form, fine. For whatever your choice, as a spiritual being you are complete.

Unhappily, most people who are fat resist the idea that they are complete, feel that there is a lack in their life, and choose food as a means of compensating for this lack. In fact, all forms of sickness and addiction—smoking, drinking, drugs—arise out of resistance and a feeling of lack. The choice of faulty substitutes to fill this lack creates misery, unhappiness, and sometimes, death.

The act of resistance to various aspects of life is a common one. You may resist criticism or disapproval. You may resist the feelings of lack and limitation. Through fear, you may resist success or being close to people. Unfortunately, the thing you resist persists because you give energy to it. If only we could all accept the truth that, as spiritual beings, we are already complete and one with God. There is no lack, no void waiting to be filled. Each of us is a full reservoir of love and abundance; and when we truly accept this fact, all we can really do is give to others. But when the belief of lack and emptiness persists, when we believe we are a void waiting to be filled, then we will always be trying to find something to fill up that emptiness.

It may surprise you to know that overweight and under-weight both come from the same mental attitude: the sense of lack. Overweight and underweight are simply two sides of the same coin: inadequacy feelings. To some degree, all of us have feelings of inadequacy but choose ways of expressing them other than gaining weight. Whatever the choice, it is a faulty substitute for the acceptance of our spiritual completeness.

Part of the pain in being fat is that the condition is so obvious. And it is astonishing how a fat person can create discomfort in others. To these observers, the fat person manifests a low self-image, and people resist this because it reminds them of their own low self-image. The low self-image projected by the fat person creates fear in others who are afraid to look honestly at themselves.

People blame food for producing fat, but we know that food doesn't make all people fat. We've all known skinny people who eat like horses and still don't gain weight. The usual answer is that it all depends upon one's metabolism. This is faulty thinking because it implies that metabolism has a mind of its own. Well, it doesn't. You, consciously or unconsciously, direct your metabolism. By raising your consciousness, you can change it.

The loss of control of the body—giving up of consciousness, if you will—begins early in life. Often the fat adult gained acceptance as a child by cleaning his or her plate. Parents, who felt guilty for depriving the child of attention, may have tried to remedy the situation with gifts of candy, ice cream, and cake. Thus, food became a substitute for attention and a symbol of acceptance, love, and affection.

Whatever satisfactions food provides, they are temporary at best. As soon as the person stops eating, his or her attention is again focused on the gnawing need. The self-doubt, the boredom and lack of fulfillment remain. So, try some more food!

These habits are established very early. My younger sister is an example. When we were very young, my parents went through a period of separation. I went to live with my great-grandmother, and my sister went to live with a well-to-do couple unrelated to our family. Despite their good intentions, my sister felt rejected and miserable. In an effort to make her happy, the couple gave her everything she asked for, including food and candy. They gave her lots of attention; but because she did not feel good within herself, no matter what she was given, it was not enough. As a consequence, she created a weight problem. She had this problem until she was in her thirties. At that time, she changed her need for food by changing her belief system. She became a Christian and gained fulfillment through her acceptance that Jesus loves her. With this new belief, she felt fulfilled. She no longer has a weight problem, and has even written a book on how to lose weight.

She is, of course, an example of what we are talking about. Our beliefs about ourselves control how we look, our form. You see, who you are is greater than your body, greater than your weight, your relationships, your religion, your politics. Who you are is bigger than your life experiences. Your life experiences are the context of your life; and because you create those experiences, you can choose to change your weight.

You have to start with the knowledge that you are complete already and totally accept that God loves you. You must avoid self-condemnation. If you believe that you and your body are the same thing and you don't like your body, you cannot like yourself. You judge yourself more severely than anyone else, and you can become the judge, jury, jailer, and ultimately, the executioner.

You have to be willing to accept yourself, your value as a person and a spiritual being, regardless of your weight. As long as you think, "I'll be okay when I'm slender," you're fighting the wrong battle. You've judged yourself unworthy, and you're trying to become good through your body. This is an impossible situation because it puts you in the position of being run by your body, by food, and by other people. You lose weight and you gain weight over and over again because you're still run by the fear that you're not complete.

Probably 30 to 40 percent of the people who come to me for counseling have weight problems, even though many of them do not come to talk about that problem specifically. But some of them do; and as I listen, I can see that, not only is fat a false substitute for love and affection, but also fat is used by many as a false protection against the fear of close relationships, particularly sexual ones. In other words, the unconscious thinking goes something like this: "If I get fat, I can keep others away and therefore avoid hurt, pain, rejection, and the other risks involved in close, open relationships." Obviously, not even fat persons are spared hurt and pain.

I recall one woman who came to me, a forty-two-year-old woman who weighed about 300 pounds. She was a very successful businesswoman and had an abundance of material things in her life; but she was miserable about her weight and low self-image. She had never married; and even though she was successful in business, most of her time was spent in preoccupation with food and weight.

As it turned out, she had, in effect, made the decision to be fat when she was seven years old. A minister's daughter, she was very pretty, a petite, blonde girl who was everybody's little darling. As young as she was, she wanted people to love her for more than just being pretty. She'd overheard people comment that she was just too cute, that she would always be some man's little darling. She sensed the implied criticism in these remarks and decided something must be wrong in being a pretty little girl. She decided that, to get and hold on to approval, she had to be something more than just pretty. So she decided that she would be intelligent, weighty in the world, a person of substance. As the years passed, she continued to concentrate on being intelligent. She literally rejected beauty as a primary value in her life and concentrated on her intellect. As she did so, she set up pressures in her life that she sought to ease through eating. As she became fat, kids teased her, and this evidence of rejection only made her feel more lonely and insecure. She began to feel guilty about eating. And the guilt just provided pressure for eating more. She'd set up the circle.

To become what she regarded as a person of "substance," she had given up, besides beauty, closeness. Actually she was afraid of closeness, for fear of being rejected. Now, when she came to me, she wanted to be intelligent and capable and prosperous, yes. But she also wanted to be slender and pretty and have men in her life. She is now approaching a willingness to risk relationships, to be willing to love—and to lose. For only those who are willing to risk in relationships are going to experience the magnificent relationship that everyone is seeking.

During counseling her consciousness and mental attitude are changing and she is beginning to reduce her weight substantially. She no longer eats each time she suffers a pang of anxiety. And if she continues as she is doing now, she will soon have this problem licked.

Food, of course, is a necessity that should be enjoyed both for its nourishment and its taste. Too often we use it as a substitute for something else. Some eat when they are happy; others, when they are unhappy. Some eat when they are bored; others, when they're angry. Some eat for sexual gratification. In all of these cases, food is being substituted for aliveness. When we're caught in this sort of cycle, it's hard to remember that food is here to sustain us and not to fulfill our psychological needs. Over and over again, we use it to fill the emptinesses in our lives.

In counseling with fat people, I find that many don't even taste their food. They might as well be chewing a styrofoam cup. They may profess a great concern with evaluating the good foods and the bad foods, but they seem to choose the fattening foods. They don't want fresh fruits and vegetables: they want meat, sugars, starches, and oils because these have more substance.

Have you ever noticed a fat family in a restaurant? There is very little conversation. Each person's attention is riveted on the food. It appears that the food isn't even tasted or chewed, but is simply shoveled down as if in an attempt to fill an insatiable need. The need, of course, is not for food, but for self-acceptance and a knowledge of one's own power.

If you change your attitude about yourself, you change your attitude about food. With this change, you can come from choice about the food you eat. Eating will no longer be compulsive. You will begin to notice how food tastes. Once you totally accept that you are complete within yourself, you can then decide and choose what you will do about weight. You can choose your form and take the steps to get there.

Skinny or fat, you are a complete being. You are greater than your body, greater than the content in your life. You are in charge of your life, not run by other people. You are a spiritual being, and as such you are in charge.

As indicated early in this chapter, food is only one of many addictions and compulsions with which many of us are afflicted. People are addicted to sex, smoking, alcohol, drugs, driving too fast—the list goes on and on. And while specific programs for each of these addictions may differ, the underlying principle is that all of these problems come about in much the same way a weight problem does. The individual is trying to use people, places, and things to fill up the feeling of emptiness. In each instance, the essential beginning procedure is the same: recognize that you are already a complete being and that God loves you. Once you can consciously accept this, you will then be able to operate from choice and get the results you want.

SELF-AWARENESS STRATEGIES AND EXERCISES

▉ OBSERVE

Notice what goes on in your mind when you get hungry. Do you eat because you are hungry, really hungry? Or are you filling some other need?

What happens when you sit down to eat? Notice if you feel you have to clean your plate, or if you tend to eat at certain times, or under certain conditions of stress.

Observe your food shopping habits. Do you buy fresh fruits and vegetables? Or do you talk yourself into "just one" piece of candy or bag of potato chips?

How do you feel about your weight? Are you waiting to get thin to be happy?

How do you feel about slender people?

▉ CHOOSE

Accept right now that you have created the form you have. If you are fat, say, "Okay, I have chosen to be fat." Look at yourself in the mirror. Really look at what you have created. Accept the fact that you have used food to try to feel complete. Bring your unconscious decisions about the form you have created to your conscious mind and choose them.

▉ GIVE UP BLAME
Quit making yourself wrong over your weight. That will get you nowhere. Even if you discover just how your childhood contributed to your choice, don't make your parents or others wrong.

▉ CREATE IT THE WAY YOU WANT IT
Get in touch with yourself as a whole, complete spiritual being. Know that you are perfect. Visualize the exact form you would like to have. Write down the exact weight. Think and experience how you would feel if you were at that weight. What problems would that bring? How would you handle them? Double think: see yourself as perfect now and perfect at the weight you think would be perfect. Be good and kind to yourself.

AFFIRMATIONS

1. I, _____, am a complete, perfect being just the way I am.

2. I, _____, choose to eat to sustain and nourish my physical body.

3. I, _____, have no need to use food to fill me up because I love myself just as I am.

10

RELATIONSHIPS START WITH YOU

Our lives are an incredible web of seemingly complex relationships. We are constantly interacting with parents, children, mates, bosses, employees, friends, and enemies. But before we can have a complete relationship with another, we must first have a complete relationship with ourselves. Before we can ever be loved, respected, supported, and adored by another, we must feel loving, respectful, and supportive of ourselves. We must correct our faulty belief systems and prop up our sagging self-images. The reason is that, as we seek unconditional love and support, our true intention is to attract to ourselves the treatment, circumstances, and people who duplicate the beliefs, images, and judgments we truly have about ourselves and life. If our belief systems and images are wrong, a relationship simply compounds our basic problem.

Fundamentally—at the spiritual level—there is only one relationship: our relationship with God. We are all one with God. Each of us is a child of God, and as such, we are all members of the same family. The big secret in life is that you must unconditionally love and accept yourself as a capable and magnificent being who willingly receives the abundance of God's gifts in all areas of your life.

On the physical level, even though we are spiritually related to every person on the planet, we are involved with only a small number of people at any one time. The overall purpose of these relationships is one of mutual love, value, and support. True, it doesn't look that way. That's because we distort our interactions with other people. Instead of offering value, support, and love, we often fear, hate, and manipulate, making ourselves and others miserable.

According to Ken Keyes in *Handbook to Higher Consciousness*, every person you meet is either your teacher or your lover. Sometimes the roles can be switched: a person can be your teacher at one time and your lover at another.

The teachers in our lives are those who challenge us, who push our buttons. They provide us an opportunity to receive value and transcend our experiences. Sadly, few of us seek them out. Our response to our teachers often is to become angry with them, and this anger is our way of trying to create guilt for them. Most of us look, instead, for persons we think will give us our own way, persons who will do what we want them to do and who won't stir up the waters. We're under the illusion that life around such people will be calm and comfortable and that we'll be okay. But that's not the way life works.

The lover in your life is a person who is totally supportive. When I love you, I totally accept you, and I'm willing for you to be all that you can be—even if it means leaving me. Your lover can become your teacher, too. You may learn from your lover some of the desirable qualities you wish to incorporate within yourself. That's an ideal, mutually loving relationship.

What happens more often is that you or your partner takes a mutually loving relationship and makes it possessive. Confronted with some new demands, you allow possessiveness to take over. When examined, possessiveness reveals itself as just another face of hate and fear. You see, we are under the illusion that life with those who give us our way will be peaceful and secure. We think we need this sort of bland conformity to make ourselves okay. But I repeat, no matter how hard we try, life never works out that way.

We are preoccupied with resisting conflict and stress. We waste our energy and spirit opposing those who disagree with us and won't give us our own way. These are the people we call "enemy," the people we don't like. We gossip about them and try to destroy them with words. This verbal murder is our "civilized" way of killing without getting ourselves killed. It's one of the subtle means of trying to control and dominate the other. Of course, it's all self-defeating, because it is a violation of the spirit of both parties.

The natural spirit of each individual is free, open, loving, and unpossessive. The success of all of our relationships is assured if the foundation is based on the True Spirit. The ideas you hold take form in your beliefs, and the nature of your beliefs will determine whether your relationships are valuable or destructive. Nothing happens in your life that does not afford some value, but the only way you can be assured of always receiving value is by transforming your relationships.

A transformed relationship is one in which there is tremendous support and love. This love and support does not mean complete agreement between the parties; rather, it means alignment. You recognize that God is your source and that the other person is not the cause of anything in your life. He or she is not the cause of your happiness or misery. He or she is not the reason you feel loved or rejected. With God as your source, you are the cause. The other person is in your life because of your transformed relationship—out of love.

The vast majority of people on this planet have untransformed relationships. These are the relationships based on possessiveness, guilt, domination, and control. We see so much of this type of relationship that we begin to think it's a natural way of life. Our choice, then, becomes whether we should try to put up with the unhappy relationship or try to discover new techniques of domination that will force it into a more acceptable form.

But a transformed relationship cannot come from a person who has not been transformed as an individual. *You* are the only one who can transform yourself. If *you* have not accepted unconditional love, abundance, and happiness—all the things that God has already given you—then there is no way someone else is going to give them to you. It may look like the other person will be able to give them to you; but if you are not transformed, your belief system will find a way to sabotage the relationship. You will turn it around because your own consciousness can't handle love. And the reason you can't handle love is because you have not accepted your own self-love, worthiness, and the God within.

The key to your individual transformation is knowing profoundly that you are the cause, the source in your own life. You achieve this knowledge by observing yourself. You will soon see that the person suppressing you could not do it if you refused to be suppressed. You will decide not to give others your power: you simply will not allow them to have it.

For such personal observations to be effective, tremendous self-honesty is required. You must see which of your relationships work and which ones don't. You may discover that you really like being alone a great deal of the time. Or you may discover that you can't stand being alone at all. As you begin to examine your relationships, you will see which ones support you and which ones don't. You will eventually see that each relationship is telling you what you think and believe about yourself at a particular moment and in a specific situation.

It is at this point that you are in the position to decide to be yourself, to say and do what you want. Others, confronted with your new honesty, may attempt to put you down. This will continue until you are comfortable with the idea that you can be who you are. If you have doubts, the other person will simply echo, or reflect back to you, your true inner beliefs about yourself. As this happens, you gain another opportunity to learn and grow. The transforming person says: "Oh, that's where I am now. I still haven't accepted that I'm worthy of saying and being who and what I want." The transforming person will not fight over an unpleasant encounter.

On the other hand, the untransformed person fights the suppressor and, in turn, is more suppressed. His or her real self is even more diminished. He or she cries: "I try something, and I'm killed for it. What's the use of trying to be my real self if I'm going to be put down for it? I just won't try anymore. I'd rather be safe." The untransformed person pays a terrible price for this illusion of safety.

You *must* recognize that, as a spiritual being, you are absolute on the spiritual level. You *must* recognize that you, through the use of your mind, create your individual life scenario. The untransformed person re-creates the same script over and over. The transformed person knows he or she may change the script at any time.

Transformed persons, observing their role as the *cause*, will spend their time working on self-love and a sense of worthiness, working on accepting more and more of God's love. They will take responsibility for their own feelings, emotions, finances, and jobs. They will know that they are not victims. Using their True Selves, they will accept the gifts that God has given them.

SELF-AWARENESS STRATEGIES AND EXERCISES

■ OBSERVE
Notice how you respond in your various relationships. Do you find you react with guilt, want to control, or try to possess?

Are you happy or unhappy with the relationships in your life? Which ones are the best? Why? Which ones are the source of conflict for you? Why?

Watch how you behave and note what you feel in each encounter. Look for patterns that will help you to understand your beliefs and attitudes.

■ CHOOSE
Whatever your responses, however you react and respond, accept that, for now, this is the way you are.

Make these conscious choices. If you always feel guilty when you are with a person, say to yourself, "I choose to feel guilty with this person." If you want to control another, say, "I choose to try to control this person." Take full responsibility for what goes on in all of your relationships.

■ GIVE UP BLAME

Quit making yourself wrong about the way you handle your relationships. You are a perfect being and one with God. This is true of others, too. You must not blame them for what happens to you. Blame of self or others only compounds the problem.

■ CREATE IT THE WAY YOU WANT IT

How would you like your relationships with others to be? Take time to form a clear mental picture of the way you would like them to be. Visualize yourself with the various people in your life. What would you like to say? How would you like them to respond? Use your imagination to create the feelings you would like to have. Write an affirmation that details the changes you would like to have in your relationships. Read it aloud to yourself often and with feeling.

AFFIRMATIONS

1. I, _____, am a unique and perfect creation of God, and all that I need in every area of my life is being given to me at the right time.

2. I, _____, am willing to know all about myself, and I accept and love all parts of myself, including
my adequacies and inadequacies.

3. I, _____, am willing to be alone with myself, and I enjoy myself completely, which brings more
love and support into all of my relationships.

11

TO POSSESS IS
TO DESTROY

The most intimate relationship in our lives is the one we have with our mate—husband, wife, lover, significant other. In this relationship, we have the perfect setting for Heaven, Hell, and all the various places in between. The relationship that can exist between two people who are willing to love and support each other unconditionally is the most sacred of all earthly unions. Such an ideal setting provides the greatest opportunity available to us to experience true ecstasy. The problem is that most people are unwilling to experience the emotions and fears that are necessary if they are to open up to the highest levels of communication and oneness.

What is required in a magnificent love relationship is that both people be committed to themselves, to one another, and to the relationship. They must each agree to handle and resolve any difficulties until each partner feels clear and light. This dedication of effort to confront and try to resolve problems is very important, because when couples split over unresolved differences, they are able to rationalize the separation and make each other wrong. If one chooses to change the form of a relationship, the move should be made only after all is clear and all wrongness is dissolved. At the end of this chapter I have included the marriage vows I use in weddings I perform. I wish to share them with you because it is the same kind of agreement or value foundation that two people may use in any intimate relationship, married or otherwise.

Probably, the number one problem people bring to me in counseling is: How can I have a truly satisfying relationship with my mate? The simple answer is that our intimate relationships are destroyed by the chronic desire to possess or suppress. This desire to possess is so prevalent that it almost seems congenital. But the desire is not natural. It comes from the mistaken beliefs we have about relationships generally.

Your relationships with others grow out of your relationship with yourself. The earliest relationship you have is with your parents, and this relationship determines how you see yourself. The way you handle and feel about these initial relationships will tend to control all of the other relationships in your life. The men in your life will be much like your father, and the women will be much like your mother. And there are the brothers and sisters. The way you related to them sets the stage for the nature of subsequent relationships with friends. These family relationships determine beliefs we have about other men and women, about closeness, about love and support.

Because beliefs create reality, the beliefs you hold as you move from your family out into the world determine the kinds of relationships you are going to have. The countless miserable relationships we see are sobering evidence of how mistaken these beliefs are.

Relationships with mates have a particular importance. If they are good and happy ones, we are strengthened to cope with the problems of the outside world. If these relationships are bad and unhappy, they will cloud and ruin whatever other kinds of successes we might have outside the relationship. The ideal relationship is one in which each partner says: "I support you for being who you are, who you are not, and who you can be. I support you in your goals and purpose in life. I support you in sharing all of your thoughts, ideas, and feelings. And I will not judge. I will not suppress. Most important, this type of sharing is sacred to me. *I am not going to bring up your sharing at some later time and use it as a weapon.*"

However, suppression lurks on the edge of every relationship; but as I emphasize again and again, you can be suppressed only if you allow it. The insidious way we get into suppression is by way of the fear of losing the other person. This fear of loss manifests itself in the desire to possess, which, in the simplest sense, is the great destroyer of all intimate relationships. For, you see, to possess you give away your power.

When you try to possess the other person, you become dependent upon that person for your love, happiness, and well-being. You forget that God is the source and that you are in control of your own life. This attempt at possession leads you to seek to change the other person because you see him or her as the source and the cause of your unhappiness. He or she resists being changed, and things just get worse. The Bible says, "For the thing which I greatly feared is come upon me, and that which I was afraid of is come unto me" (Job 3:25). As you resist your fear, you seem to get more of it.

Yet it is through releasing with love that you will be able to have the magnificent relationship you want. Our fear, of course, tells us that, if we let those we love go, if we release them, they will go away. As we begin to possess and act out of fear, the whole relationship changes and comes apart. We don't say what we want to say, we don't act the way we want to act, we don't live the way we want to live. We operate from the mistaken belief that, if we are honest and open, we will somehow lose the other person. Thus, our goals are abandoned and we dare not express ourselves. We fear that those we love will abandon us. Sometimes we get so fed up with the situation that we leave, or force those we "love" to leave us. Either way we have created the very thing we feared most: they are gone. Paradoxically, when we move from the Spirit in our relationships, we are always willing to lose the other person because we know that relationships don't end, they just change.

What we seek in possession is ownership of the person; and when we try to own a person, we often feel we must hang on to them. It's much like hanging on to an old piece of furniture. Even though we don't like it, even though it doesn't fit our needs, we feel we have too much invested in it to let it go. So we hang on to the relationship long after it has gone completely sour.

I remember my first marriage. Long after I had become fed up with the relationship, long after the realization that there was no way to save it, I still remained in it. When I became honest with myself, I realized I was hanging on to my husband because I didn't want another woman to have him. That's how stupid possession can become. Our ego works out of fear, and we give our power to the other person. Our very vocabulary reveals and confirms our beliefs. We say *my* doctor, *my* hairdresser, *my* child, *my* husband, *my* wife.

Opposite our fear-driven ego is the Spirit, our Godself. This Spirit is total love. That's what Jesus taught, and the Christ consciousness ultimately means the willingness to release everything. As you develop this Christ consciousness, it may be helpful to know that sometimes it feels like a double bind. At first we experience the sense of release, and it's pretty heady stuff. All the good things—both material and spiritual—start coming to us. But still lurking on the edge of our new happiness is our egomania, waiting to creep back into our lives. As it does, we are once again consumed with fear of loss and the desire to possess. We fear we will make a mistake and lose all of these marvelous things. Don't be discouraged. It takes practice to give up old ideas and beliefs.

When you've accepted the God within as your source and are truly in full support of yourself and who you are, you stop creating relationships with so many suppressive people and are able to deal with them in a constructive manner. When you are in full support of yourself, your mate or other intimate person may express ideas and take actions that are contrary to your ideal; however, he won't succeed in knocking you off center because you will know that he is not the cause of either your happiness or your unhappiness. You can either thank him for sharing, or you can walk out of the room.

So often we are afraid to just acknowledge his ideas or to walk out of the room because we fear that he will leave. As long as we react from the fear of his leaving, the relationship is founded on the avoidance of loss. It's not based on how you can add happiness to the relationship, or on how you can support the other, or even on how you can enhance and express yourself. Instead, you're caught up in how you can prevent the other from leaving.

In spite of what advertising, movies, and novels tell us, love and having things in common are not the real reasons for having an intimate relationship. The true grounds for such a relationship are that we chose to live our lives together and to continue, in that relationship, to expand the knowledge of who we are. We acknowledge that we both come from Spirit and intend to live out of the Spirit. Each accepts that he does not need the other. Each must be willing to give up the relationship, if giving it up truly supports the other. That doesn't mean that either one is actually going to leave, but that each is willing to let go. Freedom begets freedom. Both must be willing to acknowledge that they can handle their lives comfortably and successfully without the other. Both must acknowledge that they are in the relationship because they choose to be, because each believes that he is receiving value from that relationship. Each must be willing for the other to express his own personality and uniqueness. Each wants the other to be loved by other people, to be happy in his work, and so on. And, most important, each knows that God, and not the partner, is the source of good.

MARRIAGE VOWS

_____ and _____ have asked
(groom's name)   *(bride's name)*
us to share this day of their marriage with them. Their
vows are the foundation from which their lives together
will continue to open into ever-expanding levels of
happiness, love, health, and self-expression. Who
supports the man and woman in their marriage? (*Best
man or father of the bride steps forward.*)

Those who are now married may want to renew their
vows today, those who want to look at what's ahead may
want to take the vows, or those who are not interested in
marriage may want to look at what it means to be a
friend, for marriage is based on friendship.

The purpose of their marriage is to create a loving
support unit in which both _____ and
(groom's name)
_____ will be all they can be spiritually,
(bride's name)
mentally, and physically. Their first priority is their
relationship with God, the second is their relationship
with each other, and the third is their work and their
unique destinies. Their marriage is to enhance who they
are and what they have as single people. They have
chosen to be together in a marriage where they are safe
to express their feelings, emotions, and thoughts.

Marriage can be a great adventure when it is the outward
expression of a great love. Such a love is characterized by
compassion, passion, and courage. It makes you able to

see through to your partner's essence; willing to be in total support of your partner's well-being, goals, purpose, and spirit; and unwilling for your partner to be less than all he or she can be spiritually, mentally, and physically. Such a love requires that you be totally honest with yourself and your mate, that you ask for what you want, take action even though you are afraid, share how it is for you, and listen but leave your partner free.

Marriage is the form in which you have chosen to express and live your love relationship. To serve its purpose, your marriage must change as you change, but your unchanging commitment to love and to life will allow you both to experience and share a magnificence unknown to you before.

We accept for you, because we accept for ourselves, a love that brings out your magnificence, a love that gives you the courage to stand apart and the willingness to stand together. We accept for you a home of private retreat.

Most of all we want that, at the end of your lives on this planet, you will look into each others eyes and be able to say, "Because you have loved me, you have given me faith in myself, and because I have faith in myself, I have loved my fellow man. My life with you has been complete."

Will you join right hands. _____, look
(groom's name)
into _____'s being and repeat after me:
(bride's name)

"I, _____ love and support you,
(groom's name)

_____, for being all that you are and all that
(bride's name)

you are and all that you can be. Of all the women I

have met and known, I choose you to be my wife. I love

you, adore you, and cherish you all the days of my life."

(Repeat for bride.)

_____, what token do you give of your love
(groom's name)

for _____? (Groom hands ring to minister.)
(bride's name)

This ring is the symbol of the endless spiritual love that

links you Spirit to Spirit. _____, place this
(groom's name)

ring on _____'s finger and repeat after me:
(bride's name)

"This ring is the symbol of my unconditional love and

support."

_____, what token do you give of your love
(bride's name)

for _____? (Bride hands ring to minister.)
(groom's name)

This ring is the symbol of the endless spiritual love that

links you Spirit to Spirit. _____, place this
(bride's name)

ring on _____'s finger and repeat after me:
(groom's name)

"This ring is the symbol of my unconditional love and

support."

Inasmuch as _____ and _____
(groom's name)   (bride's name)

have agreed to the vows, by the power vested in me, I

now pronounce you husband and wife.

May I present Mr. and Mrs. _____
(groom's name)

SELF-AWARENESS STRATEGIES
AND EXERCISES

▧ OBSERVE

Start right where you are. Are you in an intimate relationship? If you are, notice what's going on. Are you
willing to share your thoughts, feelings, and ideas? Or
are you afraid that, if you express yourself fully, you will
be rejected?

If you are afraid, ask yourself what you are afraid of. Be
honest with yourself.

Now, ask yourself what your reaction is when your mate
expresses himself or herself honestly and openly. How
do you feel? Do you feel threatened or like he or she
doesn't love you anymore?

If you are not in an intimate relationship right now, ask
yourself how you feel about that.

Notice what your reaction is when you meet new people.
How do you feel about people who are open and honest?
Are you willing to be open and honest with them? If not,
why not?

▧ CHOOSE

Accept that where you are right now in relationships is
where you are. Recognize that, consciously or unconsciously, you have created that. Accept the responsibility
for your relationships. Even if they seem to be negative,

accept and choose that for right now. This is the first step in changing.

▨ GIVE UP BLAME
Whatever your situation is, accept it. Know that you need not feel guilt or make yourself or another wrong. Give up the idea that other people are responsible for your life, your happiness, your good. Say to yourself, "I choose this situation now. I am not guilty."

▨ CREATE IT THE WAY YOU WANT IT
Get clear on just what sort of relationship you want with a significant other. Be specific and know what sort of communication you want to experience. Picture yourself telling your deepest desires to the one you love without fear. See that person accepting you just the way you are. Visualize yourself accepting the other person just the way you want to be accepted.

AFFIRMATIONS

1. I, _____, accept that my right mate is in my life now.

2. I, _____, am not possessive about my mate; I lovingly give _____ the freedom and support he/she needs.

3. I, _____, easily, comfortably, and joyously support my mate to be all he/she can be, no matter how that support affects the form of our relationship.

12

CHILDREN ARE BORN CAPABLE

Our problems with children begin with our misperception of them. We tend to see our children as essentially helpless and incapable. Because the newborn comes equipped with the divine potential for perfection, it follows that each child is born with the ability to learn, to give and receive love, to feel and express. The child is born with a sense of identity because he or she arrives with all of the infinite capabilities of a spiritual being. This tiny individual arrives complete and all knowing at the spiritual level, even though he or she does not know words and cannot add one plus one. But as a mental and physical being, the child has the capacity to develop all of the motor skills, the intellect to gather and process data—in short, all of the learning skills and talents a person needs for mature development. And, above all, the child arrives ready and eager to participate. The trouble begins with us, the parents—and other members of the family—and our reasons for having children.

The ideal reason for having a child is the desire to share and support a new human being as it blossoms into a happy, loving, fully expressed adult. That's the ideal. Unhappily, people have children for reasons ranging from the sublime to the ridiculous. We all know the couple who have a child to hold the marriage together, or the husband who is desperate for a son to take over the family business. There are women who get pregnant to force marriage on a boyfriend. There are "accidents," and there are those who have children because they think society expects them to. I'm sure you could add to the list.

Of course, few parents consciously choose ridiculous reasons for having children. They are simply reacting unconsciously, out of their own unenlightened conditioning, a circumstance that is passed from generation to generation. Fortunately, it's possible to break this miserable cycle at any point. This happens when you, the adult, become conscious of the God within both yourself and your child.

In a sense, children are not ours to own and possess, but individuals entrusted into our care for a time. Kahlil Gibran puts it beautifully in *The Prophet*:

> *Your children are not your children. . . .*
> *They come through you but not from you,*
> *And though they are with you yet they belong not to*
>   *you. . . .*
> *You are the bows from which your children as living*
>   *arrows are sent forth.*

I like to say that children are just short people, but you wouldn't know it from the way we greet the child upon his arrival. The confrontation with the basic adult and the community discloses a general belief that the child is simply not a capable being. Superficially it appears that the exterior world is dedicated to teaching the child to become capable; but as we look closer, we see that, even though the child comes ready to grow, learn, and participate, we spend an amazing amount of time telling him that he is too little, too young, or too inexperienced to do anything.

Our initial responsibility is to create a loving, supportive environment where the child will be nurtured to experience his wholeness and lovableness and encouraged to follow his natural inclinations. Instead, most of our energy goes toward stifling growth in the name of protection. Of course, the child is limited by experience and size; but so often, out of our own fears and expectations, we won't allow him to try anything.

Quite early, children express desires to participate; but they're immediately told that they are too little or too young to help with the yard work or clean the house or make the bed. Is it any wonder that they, as teenagers, are unwilling to help with any of the household duties? How much better it would be if we welcomed first attempts by showing the child how to do what he so badly wants to do. This requires a certain diplomacy because every parent is familiar with the refrain: "No. I want to do it myself." But instead of the customary reply of, "You don't know how. I'll do it," we should offer our advice in small doses.

And we shouldn't be afraid to allow the child to make his own mistakes, so long as he is not personally endangered. We forget that mistakes are an integral part of the learning process. When we deny the child the opportunity to learn through mistakes, we essentially block the child's development. The child may become immobilized or decide to go around us. Then, our fears become twofold: the child is either not developing fast enough, or is growing away from us and no longer needs us.

It really doesn't take very long for us to dump our negative beliefs and fears on a child. The experts inform us that the child's major personality development occurs before the first grade. During this critical period, we impose our beliefs, even when it is clear that they haven't worked for us. Our rationalization is that there's nothing wrong with the beliefs: we just didn't apply them right. Give them to the kid; maybe he'll make them fly!

And we all know the familiar refrain: "I want my children to have a better life than I had." Now the refrain sounds loving and sensible, but unconsciously it often means: "I never got the love and approval I was looking for, so I want my child to fulfill my dreams." The problem is that we are asking the child to meet expectations that are not his, so he grows up with a misunderstanding of what constitutes happiness. He begins to believe that people, places, and things are the source of his own good; and the stage is set for him to pass on to the next generation this misperception of how life works. For as the child is brought up, so will he ultimately live. A parent who is conscious of this repetition of upbringing practices has the ability to change these insidious beliefs, and later I will discuss ways to make constructive changes.

An ideal home environment for the child is one in which the parents accept absolutely that the child is lovable and capable and is born with the latent ability to handle his own life. The parents must be willing to allow the child to make his own mistakes and to create his own successes. He should not be put down for his so-called failures, nor criticized for his mistakes. Instead, as early as possible, the child should be encouraged to learn the consequences of his actions, encouraged to take responsibility for his own life, for his own feelings. He must never be given the feeling that, if he doesn't shape up, he's going to be kicked out.

You see, children learn very early from us what is appropriate and what is inappropriate, however unrealistic our notions of appropriateness may be. Too often, they learn that it's inappropriate to express their feelings, whether these feelings are of love or of anger and hate. Thus, they store up feelings and confront their parents with pretense. Before long, no one in the family knows what any other member in the family is *really* feeling. If, in a moment of anger, a child can't say "I hate you" or "I'm angry with you," his suppressed feelings can cause severe problems in the future.

Even as we acknowledge the capability of the child, we still have a major responsibility for seeing that his home environment is safe. Admittedly, this is a tricky area and, at various stages of the child's development, there has to be a sensible position somewhere between total freedom and fearful overprotectiveness. It's a delicate line. Communicate too much fear, and the child will be scared for the rest of his life. Allow total freedom, and the child will not learn that there are *boundaries*—legal, moral, ethical—in real life. Obviously, the child needs to know that walking in front of a car is not a safe thing to do or that drinking poisons can kill. The role of the parent in these situations is not so much to instill fear but to teach the child what the consequences of these actions are, or may be. The supportive parent is there to analyze the experiences—and mistakes—that are really important to the child. The responsibility to keep the child safe is accompanied by the equally important responsibility to see that the child remains emotionally secure and confident and develops a good self-image.

In creating the loving, supportive environment, the parent should see the overall goal as creating opportunities for the child to take care of himself successfully in life and as quickly as possible. There is no reason that a child of fifteen or sixteen should not be nearing independence with the capacity to handle his own life, but he or she rarely is. We tend to keep our children dependent upon us just as our parents kept us dependent upon them. And when we keep our children dependent, we're setting them up to fail.

A supportive environment is not the same as a permissive one. In a supportive environment, there are rules, just as there are rules in the outside life you're preparing the child for. Obviously, too many rules give the child a feeling of imprisonment. But by the same token, no rules achieve almost the same result: the child is lost because he doesn't know what he can and cannot do or where he can and cannot go.

A supportive environment is one in which the rules are consistent with the conditions of real life. In short, the home ought to be run as the world operates. There are jobs that must be performed, rules that must be obeyed—and not for capricious reasons. The jobs and rules are there for the benefit of the total community and essential for it to operate amicably. In short, everyone at home has an obligation to pitch in and see that the job gets done.

Above all, in the home, the parents must be consistent. The child must be able to depend upon the parents to keep promises and follow through on what they have said. I admit this is possibly one of the hardest things for us to do. Certainly, we rarely have the chance to learn consistency from the example of our own parents. But unless we are consistent with our children, they learn nothing about *consequences*, and *consequences* are what much of life is about.

I remember years ago having difficulty getting one of my daughters to keep her room clean. One time, I would yell about what a mess the room was, but do nothing about it. The next time, I would punish her. And the next time, I would clean the room myself. And the next time I would cry. Finally, I realized that she could clean the room or not clean it, live by the rule or not. But I pointed out the *consequences*: as soon as you clean your room, you can go out to play; if the room isn't clean, you cannot go out to play.

What I was trying to teach my daughter was that the consequences in her life are not created by the authority figure in her life. The teacher does not *give* the *A* or *F* on the report card. The teacher sets up the standards, and the *A* or *F* is the consequence of the child's efforts or willingness to meet those standards. So, when the child says, "I want this," we can say, "Great, but this is what it takes to get it." In this fashion, the child has the opportunity to learn she is responsible for many of the results in her life.

I know a mother whose daughter is constantly being picked up for petty thievery—cookies from the bake shop, beer from the back of a restaurant. The mother's attitude is a casual one: "Kids will be kids." When such a child goes out into the world, she takes neither the police nor the laws seriously. She's certain the police and the law will let her off just as her mother did. Unfortunately, many of our courts confirm such a child's beliefs, and we have a country where there are still many crimes committed for which there are no consequences. Thus, many children are encouraged to think that they'll be able to "get away with it," that they'll never be caught and forced to pay. It comes as an unbelievable surprise when, one day, someone comes along and says, "You'll have to go to jail for five years for doing what you did."

If our children are to go out into the world with a realistic idea of how the world works, we as parents must set up our homes as the world is set up. There are consequences, and each of us—including the children—is responsible for the consequences. My job as the parent is to create a loving, supportive environment, but one in which my children can discover their strengths, their weaknesses, their freedom, and their barriers.

There is no joy equal to watching our children blossom into beautiful human beings. And we learn that, with enough love, we can overcome many of the mistakes we make in child-rearing. At a high level of consciousness, we see that God is the real parent of the child and that the child is in our life to enhance it. And this is the idea we should communicate to our children: that we have children because we want to be a pleasure to them, and we want them to be a pleasure to us.

Unhappily, we tend to let our children run the game. We're afraid they won't turn out right, that they will leave. We communicate that fear to them, and they respond by using our fears and guilts to dominate and manipulate us. We, the parents, become afraid to take a stand; and we, who should be in charge of the home, pass this responsibility to the children. Under these circumstances, the children become holy terrors.

So, it's up to you as a parent. You have a choice. You can create a loving environment in which your children can succeed. But there can be no success unless you have communicated that they are responsible for their actions, that they are not the only ones who exist, and that they will live all their lives in relationship to other people. The child who has learned these lessons is ready to live in the outside world.

SELF-AWARENESS STRATEGIES AND EXERCISES

▪ OBSERVE

Look back to when you were a child. Were you truly supported and loved?

Now observe how you respond to the children in your life. Are you supportive and loving? Do you welcome their growth and provide opportunities for them to become all they can be? Or do you feel fearful that they don't know enough, or that they will not love you, or that they will leave you?

Watch how you react to children. Are you comfortable with them, or would you rather they went someplace else? How do you feel when a child says, "I'd rather do it myself"?

How do you enforce the rules you have for children? How do you react to their emotions?

■ CHOOSE

Accept the fact that you are the one who chooses how you will respond to the children in your life. Make that okay with you. If you feel anger about children, say, "Okay, I choose to feel anger." If you feel fearful when a child tries something new, say, "I choose to feel fearful when this child tries something new."

■ GIVE UP BLAME

Your children respond to you, so it really does no good to blame your children for their behavior. Even if they are old enough to know better, you have had a part in setting up that behavior pattern. Don't blame the kids. Don't blame the other parent. And most of all, don't blame yourself. When you give up blame, you create a context in which change can happen.

■ CREATE IT THE WAY YOU WANT IT

Take time to write out exactly how you would like for your children to be and how you would like to respond to them. Think up various situations that cause you stress, and write out how you would change them. Visualize each of these situations, and see yourself saying and doing the things you would like to say and do. Get very clear on just how you would like it to be. Create an affirmation that says how you want it to be, and read it aloud at least twice a day.

AFFIRMATIONS

1. I, _____, easily love and support the children in my life to be all they can be.

2. I, _____, encourage the children in my life to be independent and support them in making their own decisions.

3. I, _____, joyfully accept that my job as an adult is to help the children in my life become loving, self-sufficient, independent, and fully self-expressed adults.

13

WHEN IT'S TIME TO MOVE ON

Divorce is one of the greatest causes of fear, pain, anguish, and guilt in our lives. Yet, in its simplest sense, divorce means only that the form of a relationship has changed. One or both members of the relationship no longer choose to live together in the form called marriage. The divorce results in a legal and physical separation which has two sides: it usually brings out sadness and fear in the participants, but it is also a chance for a new life. The fear of loss, which underlies all of the negative emotions in a divorce, stems from confusion about the source of our good. We are never separated from the source, from our power, but our power can be used constructively or destructively, to win or to lose. Your belief system determines whether you will use the power constructively or destructively. You have the choice.

When we marry, we hope for agreement and closeness. Marriage is, in fact, probably the greatest opportunity in the world for people to experience love and expansion. But when our belief systems are based on faulty understanding, marriage also becomes an opportunity for hate and contraction. Where the trouble begins is with our tendency to believe that, when someone lives with us, we will control, or have power over, him or her. We also believe that we will be safe and secure because we'll have someone to solve our problems.

That's not the way it works. In fact, at the beginning of each new relationship, in marriage or not, we have no way of knowing whether we will really grow together or whether we will grow apart. If we understand that our security lies within ourselves, we have a much better chance for a successful, happy marriage. If, instead, we look to people, places, and things for our well-being, we are almost certain to have disruptive relationships and marriages that end in misery and divorce.

As we study divorces, we discover that some of them occur needlessly, simply because the partners don't have the know-how to handle the mechanics of daily living. In such instances, the two people involved may truly love each other, but they fail to have a magnificent relationship either because they have never learned the skills of relationships, or because their belief systems are such that, when they have something good, they destroy it. These marriages can be saved. The couple, if they are willing, can learn the proper skills. They can do whatever is necessary to rid themselves of the destructive beliefs that deteriorate their relationship. It is these people who benefit from constructive counseling and therapy and the self-searching that is necessary to achieve the goal.

But how do you recognize one of these salvageable marriages? Say you are contemplating divorce. You look around you and ask yourself: "If all of these other things that are destroying the marriage—the kids, the in-laws, the money, the garbage—if all of these things were handled and the problems taken away, would I want to be in the marriage?" If the answer is truly "yes," then clean up the mess. If the answer is "no," then get out, because you're just kidding yourself.

And it's easy to kid yourself. I know. Once I thought the problem in my marriage was that my husband was not as conscious and aware as I was. So, he went to an awareness seminar. As soon as he went to the seminar, I discovered that I was afraid he would become more aware and I would have no justification for leaving. I saw then that I really didn't want to be with him, that I was seeking justifications for leaving.

You see, on occasion, it is simply time to move on. Either one or both of you may have gained value and learned from the marriage, but now you are moving in different directions. You choose a different form for your relationship. You may continue the relationship as friends, but it is time for you to live your lives separately. There is no right or wrong in this: it just is. And it's far better to move on than to try to stay where both of you will be unhappy.

Sometimes one partner in a marriage wants to be there and the other does not. My observation is that the one who professes to want to be there doesn't *really* want to be there, either. The situation obviously is not working for him or her, and he or she is in more pain than happiness. But he or she is afraid to tell the truth and change the situation. A marriage can't be right for one partner and not for the other. It absolutely has to be right for both, or it doesn't work for either and somebody's lying.

Another kind of divorce comes out of the circumstance where there should never have been a marriage in the first place, where two people married, not out of love, not out of just wanting to be together, but out of need. In such marriages, usually one of the partners is looking for a strength in the other that he, himself, lacks. Often the "weaker" member gains the strength coveted in the other and, having got what he wants, discards the other.

The fact is that, if we marry for survival, we usually foredoom the marriage; because if we follow the normal life process of expanding ourselves, we'll simply outgrow the "need" we saw in the marriage in the first place. Of course, some people try to preserve marriages by remaining weak because they know any achievement of mastery will destroy the relationship. That's the consequence of trying to build a relationship on powerlessness.

It is possible in very positive relationships for each of us to gain from the other. By means of a process similar to osmosis, we absorb strengths and abilities from each other. Modifications occur in our mutual behaviors, but neither one takes and then destroys. In such relationships, strengths are loved and admired rather than resented and coveted.

All of this *can* happen in a marriage created out of need, but it doesn't happen very often. What usually happens is that the partners have all of these expectations as to what marriage is going to do. Marriage is going to solve all of their problems. When they discover on the morning after that they're still the same person they were the day before, disillusion sets in. Refusing to confront their own responsibility, they begin the familiar refrain: "I'm still unhappy, so it must be you."

In counseling I ask those contemplating divorce: "What do you think single life is going to give you?" The answer usually is: "At least I can be myself." My response to that is: "Be yourself in the present situation, and you will find that you will either stay in the relationship or you won't. What you do then won't be the effect of the other person."

What people, in effect, are saying is: "I have to be divorced to be free. I have to be divorced to be myself. I have to be divorced to have fun, to be healthy." The irony is that people essentially give the same reasons for divorce as they do for marriage. The problems you have today were yesterday's solutions. Thus begins the cycle of going from place to place and person to person to find yourself. The place to find yourself is within you, not somewhere else or with someone else.

Starting where you are right now, you may remain married or become divorced. But that's not the central issue. The issue is: "Am I a complete person and am I fulfilled? Am I satisfied? Do I feel lovable and capable? Am I a successful human being?" Those questions can be answered in or out of marriage.

Now the ideas I have expressed here are guidelines and are not absolute. *They are not your answers.* The answers are your responsibility. What I can do, though, is to provide a way to look within yourself so that you can trust your own judgment.

First, you must change your attitude about mistakes. Those decisions that look like mistakes are really guideposts and opportunities for you to evaluate where you are, what your belief systems are. In this sense, it's impossible to make a mistake, because each decision is a learning experience. This does not give you license to be irresponsible, because the purpose of these decisions is to heighten the sense that you are responsible for everything that happens in your life. But I would hope that you would be able to approach the decision areas in your life with a sort of divine nonchalance, firm in the knowledge that you are a spiritual being and, as such, are a magnificent, lovable, capable person, whether you are married or not.

A terrible consequence of failure in spiritual self-recognition is the guilt we create by thinking we have made wrong decisions and that we are somehow bad, not capable, not intelligent. These feelings perpetuate self-hatred and doubt. Remember, the mind is a servomechanism that will perpetuate the negative ideas we feed it. There's no way guilt feelings can shape anybody up.

Three questions that will drive you crazy in making decisions of any kind are:

1. Did I do the right thing?
2. Am I doing the right thing?
3. Will I do the right thing?

The only place you can really look for answers is within your heart, within yourself. Yes, even if there are no mistakes, you are accountable and must own up to your own consequences. Yet, things are simply not as significant as we make them. You will survive if you are married five times, ten times. So what?

What I ask you to look at in making a decision about divorce is whether your marriage relationship is nurturing to you. Are you alive or are you dying? Are you physically well or ill? Do you want to be there or not? If the children weren't there, would you be there? Do you really assert your own feelings? Or are you afraid of your mate?

Is there violence in the relationship? Physical and emotional violence in marriage come from suppressive individuals, people not experiencing their spirit, who try to squash all of those around them. To remain in such an atmosphere, which can result from a foolish love of suffering, is to buy into such suppression. You must get away for your own safety and the safety of your children.

Also, examine the various kinds of fears people have about

getting out of a marriage. Remember that beliefs create your reaction to life. They create your fears, and they create your well-being. Some of the common fears about divorce are: "I won't be able to rear the children properly alone." "I'll never find anybody else to love and live with and will be alone the rest of my life." "Divorce is a sin, and I'll be consumed in the fires of Hell." And on and on.

As for the children, a single, happy parent is a more positive influence than two miserable ones. But if a single parent fears the children will become delinquents, the kids will play upon these fears, making them self-fulfilling prophecies.

What about being lonely? Loneliness can occur in marriage or out of it. Again it's a question of your belief system, your belief in your own completeness.

And what about sin? One of the most punishing beliefs that people have about divorce is that it is a sin. Let's look at that word "sin." It comes from the Greek and was a term used in archery. When an archer missed the mark, he was said to have "sinned." That's all it means: to miss the mark. The Bible tells us (Romans 6:23) that the wages of sin is death. When you see that the original contest was war, that meant that an archer who consistently missed his target was likely to get killed. So, in that sense, the statement is true. But through poor translations, we have come to associate the word "sin" with guilt and condemnation.

One of the seeming paradoxes is that, while we are already complete, we are also involved in the process of completion. And it is because of this process that we learn from the actions we call mistakes. We are not judged for our learning experiences. The important thing is not to become paralyzed by fear, but to move ahead and to continue to learn. God's verdict is already in, and it's "not guilty."

Very often the person contemplating divorce or the person who is divorced is intimidated by friends, parents, in-laws, children, acquaintances. You will discover that *you* feel guilty because *they* do not approve. How do you handle their disapproval?

You must first acknowledge that they are reacting to you out of their own belief systems. Where marriage is concerned, we reward endurance. We give prizes for the length, not the quality, of the relationship. When a couple has been married for sixty years, we give them a prize, even if fifty of those years were, by most standards, intolerable. We need to give prizes for the quality of marriages, not for their longevity. Longevity of marriage is not necessarily prizeworthy, or even noteworthy, when you consider that many long marriages may be the work (literally!) of cowards, not courageous people. If the couple mentioned above sustained a mutually nurturing relationship for sixty years, then they, indeed, have at once earned and created their reward.

What others think of you, to paraphrase the title of this book, is none of your business. They are very concerned about what their friends, in-laws, and relatives think of *them*. But none of that is really your concern. You must make decisions based upon your own needs and your own wants. You must trust in your own judgment. Others may doubt your judgment because there are no two people with the same reality. When you do something contrary to their belief system, that act plugs them into their fears. But people whose marriages are secure are not threatened by someone else's divorce.

One problem that usually arises in divorce is that the two people continue to play roles in each other's life, particularly if there are children involved. The first feeling in divorce is: "Now that person is out of my life." But more often, he or she is not and probably will be involved, to some degree, in the rest of your life. These continuing relationships can be, and often are, very bitter.

In our fantasy we would like the divorced mate to tell us, in effect, that he or she sees now what a big mistake the divorce was and what a wonderful and magnificent person we are. It rarely happens that way. But it is well to remember that, if you wanted approval from your mate while you were married to him or her, you're still going to seek that approval after you are divorced. In that situation, the children become pawns, either to justify our lifestyles or to put down the divorced mate's lifestyle.

Looking to the divorce to make yourself right is a mistake. A divorce won't alleviate what you think is wrong with you. Your former mate will be there to remind you of all kinds of negative things in your life. Instead of plugging into what he or she says is wrong with you, simply allow his or her opinions to be just that. If you are looking to your former mate for approval, you may or may not get it. So, instead of resisting, simply allow him or her to be the way he or she is. Recognize that you don't have to play his or her game; otherwise, you will simply perpetuate the hostility game.

The thing to do is to handle your former mate as you would like to be handled. Pray for him or her in the sense that you wish him or her well. That will nourish your own life. Don't forget that you were a partner in a marriage and are at least half responsible and that there are no victims, just volunteers. So, as you handle the situation maturely and responsibly, you will feel good within yourself, regardless of what your former mate says or does.

Then, there's the painful problem of how do I tell the children. You must not lie. When a parent leaves the relationship, tell the children the truth. Don't try to make the children hate the parent who has left. Don't try to present the facts to justify you and thus win the children over to your side. That's immoral. The children will believe what you say: that the other parent abandoned them, didn't love them. The tragedy is that the children will then use this faulty belief system to create their own adult relationships. And so the vicious circle will continue.

If you really love your children, let them know that the problem is between you and your mate, that it has nothing to do with how either of you feels about them. You cannot make the children take sides or judge. Both parents must release the children. Try to tell them truthfully what is going on, but both of you must continue to love and support them to the fullest extent that you can. In that way, the children can be nurtured in the situation, rather than destroyed by it. Children are strong and can handle a lot, if they are loved, supported, and told the truth.

When children are lied to, they allow their imaginations to take over in an effort to determine what's true and what isn't. Under these circumstances, there's no way for them to figure the truth. Consequently, they will support the parents in their weaknesses and inadequacies. If told the truth, the children can be pillars of support to the parents' insecurities.

So we come back to the beginning. Divorce is a change in the form of a relationship. Because people change in their realization of themselves, even the form of the best relationships is constantly changing. People are not static. They are expanding. And if the relationship has fulfilled its purpose, then it is time to close that book and move on, remembering that no one is right and no one is wrong. God is the source. Learn from it, grow with it. Examine your beliefs and, as you move to your next relationship, ask what you want it to be. I reiterate that *you* create your life the way you want it, and you do that either consciously or unconsciously. So increase your level of consciousness and create conscious, responsible relationships.

SELF-AWARENESS STRATEGIES AND EXERCISES

■ OBSERVE

If your marriage is unhappy, ask yourself: "What are the problems that I see as causing my unhappiness?" Make a list of these problems.

Now ask yourself: "If all of these problems went away, would I truly want to be married to this person? Do I feel my essence is being squashed? Do I feel alive or do I feel like I'm dying?"

Ask yourself what you expect single life to give you. Are your expectations realistic, or are you still looking for something or someone else to solve your problems?

Ask yourself what you fear most when thinking about divorce. Are your fears real or false fears?

■ CHOOSE

Go ahead and give yourself permission to feel what you feel and fear what you fear. Just look at it and notice how you are at the moment. Accept your attitudes just the way they are.

▥ GIVE UP BLAME

Don't make yourself wrong for wanting a divorce or not wanting a divorce. Don't make your mate wrong for wanting a divorce or not wanting a divorce. Don't blame your children, your finances, or anything for your situation. Recognize that the power is neutral and can be used constructively or destructively.

▥ CREATE IT THE WAY YOU WANT IT

Make a list of ten changes you want in your relationship. Now take each item and see what you can do to bring about a change in yourself to allow these changes to happen. Write a detailed affirmation that spells out exactly what you want. Read it aloud at least twice a day.

AFFIRMATIONS

1. I, _____, am the expert on my own life. I trust my own decisions.

2. I, _____, have the right and the ability to create my life exactly the way I want it.

3. I, _____, know that God's judgment is in and that I am not guilty.

14

EVERYBODY CAN WIN

For all the complexity of intimate relationships we have at home, most of us actually spend the biggest part of our time at work. As a consequence, the relationships we have with those at work take on tremendous importance. In most instances, our work occurs in organizations of some kind where there is a structure, a hierarchy. While I shall be discussing the business organization primarily, the same principles apply to all organizations, including those at school and church, as well as unions, service clubs, and babysitting co-ops, for in each organization, there is the central problem of boss-employee or superior-subordinate relationships.

Ideally, the business setting offers absolutely magnificent opportunities for people to experience that they are capable, to gain self-esteem and self-appreciation, and best of all, a sense of being a productive person. When the game called business is properly played, the players are continually challenged to use their abilities and have the opportunity to grow. What too often happens is that the business situation becomes one in which people are, in a sense, killed—their abilities, stifled; their self-confidence, undermined; their self-worth, destroyed. Does that sound too harsh? Just look around you. People are continually on sick leave. They can't get along with the person next to them. The employer finds reasons to make the employee wrong, and the employee finds reasons to make the employer wrong. The one in charge is afraid to give the subordinates too much power or support for fear that they will want more money and more control. On the other hand, the employees are afraid to support the employer too much for fear he will become more successful and powerful and will refuse to meet their needs. So what happens is that most businesses are concerned with avoiding loss rather than with allowing everyone to win.

Enlightened management is concerned with creating a work environment that is nurturing, supportive, fun, and prosperous for all involved. In fact, bosses have a tremendous opportunity to create a positive work environment. Whether the organization is making a product or providing a service, the boss's overall purpose can be fulfilled only when the employees are able to expand their talents and abilities. In such a work environment, people learn how to communicate, how to work with others of different backgrounds and temperaments, and how to enjoy being members of a team.

In business seminars I conduct, I refer to business as a game. Like a game, a business has its rules and purpose. It has a starting point, a finish point, various objectives, and players. As in a game, the players all want to win. Every individual in the business, from the president to the janitor, is playing the game. Each has a different role, which he must play well if the team is to win the game. There is no essential human difference between the president and the janitor. Fundamentally, both are lovable and capable people. The biggest difference is a functional one: the president is willing to assume the responsibility for the whole team, while the janitor is willing to assume responsibility for physical maintenance. The various levels of positions within the business have little to do with *better* or *worse*. Each is a necessary function for the operation of the business.

A business is like a racing shell where the coxswain steers the boat and gives the orders to those rowing. He tells them when to stroke and sets the pace. If each oarsman does his part, the team reaches its destination and wins the race. A business where things are not working reminds me of a boat in which the oarsmen are arguing with one another. Some are pulling their oars in the right direction, and others are pulling in the opposite direction. In their frustration, oarsmen, members of the team, fight against the leader and among themselves. And the leader may not even know where the boat is going.

A lot of businesses are like that. They're a mess. People working there are not on the same team, not supporting one another. They are totally concerned with avoiding loss and with making others wrong.

In the business seminars I conduct, I try first to establish that a business is a game, a game in which all of the team members want to win. What I so often find is that administrators don't even know the purpose of the organization: they don't know what direction the boat is going. Some think the game is one of paperwork. Others think it's being on time. Some think it's an ego game, where one player must have more power than another. And for many, the game is merely one of survival. So really none is on the same team.

If the organization is to function in a win environment, it all has to start with the boss. The person at the top is the one who creates, monitors, and maintains the environment. The boss has the responsibility of making certain that other team members know what the organizational purpose is, know what the goals are and are in agreement with them, and understand the individual reward for being there, understand that they are winning.

Now, how do we define the purpose of an organization? My premise is that everything in life is set up as a spiritual opportunity; therefore, the essential purpose of a business or of any other organization is for its participants to experience enlightenment. The secondary purpose is to create a service or a product for the community and an opportunity for members of the organization to make a livelihood.

When you see the organizational purpose as a spiritual opportunity, you (boss or employee) can transcend life by seeing that everything in life—your job, your money, your relationships—all come out of your level of spiritual consciousness, your own intention. Such awareness challenges the barriers and obstacles and makes possible mastery of your life. And that means mastery of business and organizations. Organizations will work when you know how to make them work.

An enlightened manager is a person who has effectively handled her relationship with herself and feels sufficiently complete within herself to allow the same space for the others working on the team or in the organization to expand and enjoy self-confidence. A job setting that meets these conditions is one in which everyone wins and prospers, one where people invest their time and effort because they love it.

An unenlightened manager is one who has not effectively handled his relationship with himself and sees the job setting only as a place to get a job done. He doesn't see the job setting as a place for people to grow, to make and correct errors, as a place for people to be supported in their mistakes, as well as in their successes.

Unfortunately, in our society, we've been conditioned not to work, but to try to get out of working. Too bad, because I find that the happiest people on the planet are those who are working, not just going to a job but really working. The unhappy people are those who are on welfare or being taken care of, either publicly or privately. Another unhappy group are those so wealthy that they have no need for making a livelihood and have lost their purpose in life.

In an organization, there are the inevitable job descriptions, a breakdown of the overall function so that each person has a specific slot and place. Whatever the slot, the person who is in it needs to feel the satisfaction from a job well done. She must feel that she is productive and is making a contribution to the organization and to the community. You see, actually, people want to make a contribution to other people's lives. But they forget that and think what they really want is for other people to contribute to their lives. That's welfare, which is predicated on the premise that what people really want is money.

Well, it's pretty clear that people want something more than money. Otherwise, welfare would work. What people want is a sense of their own capability and recognition by others that they are capable. And the best way to feel capable is still to handle a job and complete it. I would guess that less than 5 percent of the people in the world consistently complete a project they have started. People who don't experience successful completion can't experience satisfaction.

Most of the people in the world are not conscious of their

capability. They have no idea what enlightenment is all about. In many instances, they've never succeeded at anything and don't feel capable. This is the nature of the employment pool to which organizational employers go to fill jobs. People are, so to speak, hired off the street and it's on the job that all their inner chaos and problems surface.

If you're starting a business, make certain you hire only players, only individuals who are willing to support the purpose, goals, and intentions of your organization—and who have the ability to do the job that is there for them to do. As an employer, do not compromise those values within yourself. Set up training programs that offer opportunities for people to communicate, to share, to grow, to air their gripes, to retain their identity. Monitor to make sure that people feel rewarded for what they are doing. In short, once you've hired a person, you have a responsibility to create an environment where he or she can succeed.

The difficulty with the large existing organization is that it rarely deals with the individual at the heart level, the level where appreciation and recognition are needed. Large organizations spend millions of dollars on personnel and training programs, and much of it is wasted. A nice environment with good design, plenty of color, and Muzak is not exactly the answer.

Every training program, to be effective, must start with the need for individuals to assume personal responsibility for their own lives. Only when this responsibility exists will individuals take responsibility for their jobs, for their relationships, for their place on the boat and in the game, responsibility for the team's winning the game and for the boat's going where it is supposed to go. I have found in my training programs that you actually have to first train individuals to assume personal responsibility. When they know how to do that and learn the organization rules, they can learn how to win. For large organizations, such training takes lots of time and is expensive.

Many organizational training programs avoid the psychological and spiritual aspects of the individual. The organizations think that those on the job are concerned only with better benefits, more money, shorter hours, longer weekends. Of course, people who have learned to handle their own relationships with themselves and love their work are not concerned about hours. For them, their work becomes play.

People say to me: "But what about the unions? They wouldn't let people work long hours just because it was fun." My answer is that the unions were created out of good intent, out of the desire to provide better pay and working conditions for individuals who were being taken advantage of by unenlightened management. It was true that these exploited people were not being represented or taken care of; but as the unions organized the people and became institutionalized, they lost sight of what provides real value to the individual. Many of the unions and management, too, forgot that what a person really gets value from is doing the job well, being pleased with the results of his or her work. Certainly, employees want financial remuneration, but they also want appreciation and acknowledgment, an opportunity to expand, and a relationship to the completed product. They want to see the product as a real, positive thing. Instead, we've proceeded on the assumption that more sick leave and more vacation days were the keys to job happiness. And by doing so, we have supported the notion that people really don't want to work, that you can't expect too much from them.

I know this is false, because I have learned in my own organization that people are capable, willing, and anxious to

go to the limit—even if they are volunteers without pay—
when their needs for recognition are met and when they feel
that what they are doing is contributing to other people's
lives.

One result of the faulty approach is the presence of millions
of unhappy jobholders. Another result is that the productivity
of American workers—hitherto the most productive in the
world—has been declining in recent years.

We must recognize that what people really want out of the
work relationship is not peace and tranquillity, not higher pay
and shorter hours, not something for nothing. At the bottom
line, they want love, understanding, support, and freedom to
be all that they can be.

As an employer—a boss, if you will—perhaps the most
important thing I have learned is that my employees are not
working for me. My role is to keep doing my job so well that
they will have jobs, income, satisfaction, and fulfillment in
what they are doing. In reality they are, or should be, working
for themselves, even though it is my organization that hires
them. In a sense, I'm really working for them. In another
sense, it's a joint venture: they support me so that I can go out
and create and start things so there will be more ways for
more people to experience themselves as capable beings. Ideally, the boss is the person who creates the game that everyone
can play and win.

With the typical cross-wired thinking we have, we think
the boss *runs*, that everybody works for the boss and he gets
all the goodies and the workers get the leftovers. Workers are
told what to do in every detail. They are often treated like
idiots and, predictably, often respond as if they were incapable of good judgment.

The enlightened boss is one who gets people to see that

they *can* do the job. He is the person willing to take responsibility for his job, whatever it may be. When the two work together with a common goal and purpose, everybody wins.

SELF-AWARENESS STRATEGIES AND EXERCISES

■ OBSERVE

Look at your place of work or at the organizations to which you belong. Notice who is in charge. How do you feel about that person? Are you comfortable with his or her authority? Do you feel that he or she is supportive or suppressive?

Now look at your relationship with those who work for you, or those over whom you have authority. How do you feel about them? Do you encourage them to be all they can be, or are you fearful that they may take your job?

When a problem arises, do you communicate honestly and openly, or do you avoid the confrontation or call it something else? What are your reactions?

■ CHOOSE

Whatever is going on in your work relationships you must accept responsibility for. Choose now to accept that responsibility. Choose to feel just what you feel in various situations and make that okay with you. If you're in a nonsupportive enviroment, say, "I choose to work here now." If you fear that someone else may get your job, say, "I choose to be afraid that he or she may get my job."

■ GIVE UP BLAME

Don't make others wrong for what is going on in your organization. They are not responsible for your life; you are. If you're in an uncomfortable place, so be it. Don't make yourself wrong either, for that will only compound the problem. Remember, you are in control of your own life. You have the opportunity to create it the way you want.

■ CREATE IT THE WAY YOU WANT IT

Make a list of the things you want changed in your organization. Use this list to visualize exactly the way you want it. Picture yourself in the various situations. See yourself responding in the way you want to respond. Imagine just how you will feel when you respond the way you want. Picture how it will be when the changes come about. How will you act? What will you say? What will others say to you? Write an affirmation that details these changes. Put it where you will see it and say it often.

AFFIRMATIONS

1. I, _____, accept responsibility for my organization, knowing that all my actions are for the best of all concerned.

2. I, _____, gladly accept the support of those I work with, knowing that each of us is in our right place.

3. I, _____, totally support those above and those below me in my organization to be all they can be.

15

SEXUALITY: ASK FOR WHAT YOU WANT

Sexual pleasure is God's way of giving you an opportunity to love and be loved. Sex is not a way of *getting* anything. It is a way of giving and of totally experiencing yourself and all of your beauty and magnificence.

Yet, there's probably no area of our lives in which there's as much confusion as there is in sex. At the turn of the century, sex was regarded as a shameful necessity, a matter to be discussed only in whispers. And these whispers held that carnality was largely the province of the male. It was okay for men to enjoy sex, but not with their wives. Sex for wives was the unpleasant means by which children were conceived. The bedchamber was surreptitiously regarded as a room for necessary occasions of unhappiness. And if, by chance, the woman enjoyed the sexual experience, it was a guilty secret she had best keep to herself.

In the past decade, the discussion of sex has been brought out of the bedroom into the women's magazines and onto the TV screen. There is a new openness about sex, and mates take their complaints to an army of therapists, who not only assure them that sex is okay but counsel them in its techniques.

Orgasm has become one of women's rights, and many men view their new responsibility of female pleasuring as a burden.

Though there appears to be a 180-degree turn in publicly expressed sexual attitudes, there is still tremendous evidence that things are not yet quite perfect in the privacy of the bedroom. I know this simply from my own counseling experiences. Sex may be ecstatic or demoralizing. It may be terribly disappointing and even painful. There is the opportunity for complete pleasure, joy, and oneness with another. There is also the opportunity for total rejection, misery, frustration, and warfare. Unhappily, the bedroom is still a battleground for many people.

Through my counseling, I find that many people go into sexual therapy thinking that, if they are secure in their sex lives, they will be secure in the rest of their lives. Obviously, this is putting the cart before the horse, for the life that is secure outside the bedroom is rarely insecure there. That's why the preoccupation with physical techniques may be a waste of time.

I'm thinking now of a man I've counseled for years. I had known this man socially, and I'd noticed in social situations that he was totally preoccupied with sex. No matter what the conversation, he always brought it around to sex with joking flirtations. Yet, in every sexual encounter with women, he experienced impotence. He thought that somewhere there was a woman with whom he would not be impotent and who would make him feel secure about himself. This man allowed his sexual impulses to run his life to the extent that he neglected the rest of his life.

After much counseling, he has now accepted the fact that his sex organ is not going to make or break him as a person, and the result is that he is paying more attention to the rest of his life. He is beginning to enjoy fulfillment in his professional and financial life and, to his surprise, his sex life is becoming satisfying and fulfilling, too.

It is hard for each of us to accept the fact that, if we are not secure within ourselves, there's no chance we'll be secure in our sex lives, in our business lives, or with our mates or children.

Essentially sex is a form of communication. It is a form of physical *and emotional* expression whereby we and our partner pleasure our bodies. Sex *can be* merely a physical act and, for many people both in and out of marriage, that's all it is. But with the added dimension of true love, it can be a spiritual expression of ecstasy for two beings joined in a cosmic oneness.

While sex is a form of communication, this communication is often blocked by hostility and misunderstandings on the part of either one or both parties. One of the greatest difficulties I find among those who come to me for counseling is that so many sexual partners cannot discuss their sexual problems with each other. They can discuss them with their counselors or therapists but are mute on the subject when they are in the bedroom. Oh, they discuss them *nonverbally* with displays of anger, coldness, aloofness, or tears, but find it impossible to verbalize their disappointments or dissatisfactions.

To have a satisfactory sexual relationship, you must listen to your body speak to you, know what you want, and be sufficiently trusting to ask your partner for it. And you must be willing to give your partner what he or she wants. Both of you, as consenting adults, are seeking a mutuality of the highest good. If you do not see yourself as a lovable and capable being, you will be insecure about your sexual needs and will not be willing to pleasure and be pleasured by your mate.

It's what we don't say that creates so many of our sexual problems. We must not be afraid to ask for what we want and accept completely that it's perfectly okay to enjoy the pleasure of our own bodies. Each must be willing and open with the other, be willing to be vulnerable and exchange communications in which there are no withholds. There may be a place for mystery in courtship, but there's no place for mystery in the sexual relationship: complete honesty must be the rule.

But telling the truth takes courage because you truly have to give up the need for approval. Hiding your sexual needs and desires from your partner only perpetuates unhappy games. If your game is to deprive yourself sexually, when your partner asks what you want, you won't even know. Or you will refuse to tell, will make some smart-aleck remark, or even start a fight so that you both end up with your backs turned to each other and go to sleep in unsatisfied, self-righteous anger.

Self-righteousness has absolutely no place in loving sex. You must give up making yourself or your partner right or wrong. The bed is not the place to get even or to victimize yourself or another. You must be willing to communicate openly and freely with your partner. This means sharing your fears, doubts, wants, and pleasures. Be compassionate with yourself and with your partner. Be committed to your own joys, to his or her joys, and to creating a loving and support-ive environment.

You must affirm your acceptance of your body as God's gift to you; and the more you are willing to accept your body as God's gift, the greater will be your sexual gratification and the greater the mutuality of ecstasy with your partner in an act that can and should transcend the physical.

I find, through listening to those I am counseling, that another common reason for sex problems is that often one or the other partner is not using sex primarily for the purpose of sex. A partner may be using sex to prove himself right, to make the other person wrong, to assert his ownership or possession, or to hurt the other person—and himself. If sex is used for other than what it is, inevitably the consequences will be disastrous.

Sex, like the rest of life, is God-given, and as given, it's all we need. If our sexual experiences are distorted, it's because our own attitudes are distorted.

As I noted earlier, the behavior you express outside the bedroom is the behavior you will express inside the bedroom. You bring your lovingness or your hostility, your security or your insecurity with you. The way you express yourself outside the bedroom becomes more pronounced in the bedroom. Your clothes are gone. There are no barriers to hide behind. You are vulnerable. You are at the mercy of your partner.

Under these circumstances, each sex partner is vulnerable. What we usually do when we feel insecure and exposed is to play a defensive game. We try to keep the other partner guessing and then really get upset when he or she doesn't guess right. If the other partner asks in frustration, "What is it you want?" we reply, "Even if I told you, you wouldn't give it to me."

Of course, when we use sex as a means of punishing the other, it is a device for punishing ourselves. And it all comes from the belief that other people are the source of our good rather than that the Infinite Spirit is the source of all good. What we do is to give up the opportunity for a beautiful sexual experience with a loved and loving one when the only thing we really ever need to give up is the idea that we don't have the opportunity.

Many of our sexual distortions derive from our fantasies. All of us have fantasies about sex with parents, siblings, romanticized figures. I am confident that fantasies derive from the profound desire within all of us to love everybody. Fantasies are natural and not wrong, but people perceive them as nasty, dirty thoughts. They feel guilty about them and allow them to block the way to a natural, loving, sexual relationship. After all, in its simplest sense, sex is an expression of the godly need to love, to express, to pleasure and enjoy.

So, many people have never had a satisfying sexual relationship. They always think it's the other person's fault. They go from mate to mate, from relationship to relationship looking for the ideal sexual experience. And they never realize that the barriers to satisfaction are their own beliefs, their own withholds, their own fears of asking for what they want. If they can overcome these barriers with one person, they will open themselves up to more loving, supportive relationships and give themselves permission to enjoy themselves sexually. They will know that their fantasies are not bad, that they don't have to be acted out, although doing so may be perfectly acceptable with a loving, supportive mate.

One of the difficulties in discussing our sexual desires with our partners is the fear that we will not only be rejected but ridiculed. A necessary condition to a loving relationship is an agreement between the partners that neither one will condemn or judge what the other asks or says. Now you may not want to do what is asked of you, and that is your prerogative; but you do not chastise or put down your sexual partner for his or her fantasy. Similarly, you refuse to be intimidated by the other's sexual beliefs; for that is suppression in that you give power to the other person and life then becomes a game of domination and avoiding domination, of manipulation and avoiding manipulation.

Sex is great, but you bring your mind and its attitudes to bed with you. And if your attitudes are ones of evaluating and judging your performance, you will judge the performance of your mate. As I have said over and over in this book, you either see the world as a supportive place or as a place out to get you. When you accept the world as supportive, you will allow yourself to experience the good things in it—and that includes sex.

If you are saying "no" to your own sexuality, the universe will say "no" to you through your sex partner. If you're hooked on getting approval, you'll be locked into performance, orgasm, appearances, partner comparisons, and on and on.

You must affirm that sex is all right for you and that God wants you to enjoy your body, to lovingly experience yourself and your loved ones, and without barriers or the need to hurt, or to get even, or to make wrong or right. You must accept that the bedroom is not the place for game playing in the negative sense of that term. Accept the bedroom as the opportunity for transcending love.

SELF-AWARENESS STRATEGIES AND EXERCISES

■ **OBSERVE**

Notice your beliefs about sex. When someone mentions sex, how do you react? Do you feel awkward and afraid?

Are you comfortable with your own body and with your own desires, or do you feel somehow that you're wrong? Do you feel guilty about sex?

Are you willing to ask for what you want in a sexual relationship, or do you hope your partner will read your mind?

■ CHOOSE
Whatever your feelings are at this time, choose them. If sex embarrasses you, accept that you are embarrassed about sex at the moment. If you feel guilty, say, "I choose to feel guilty now." If you really want your partner to read your mind, admit that to yourself, and choose it. Consciously tell yourself that you choose whatever beliefs you have about sex.

■ GIVE UP BLAME
Sex is one of the areas in which we are most likely to blame ourselves for our feelings. Such guilt will accomplish nothing positive. Give it up now. It's also easy to blame others. Your parents may be the ones who gave you the ideas you now have about sex, but you are responsible for your attitudes today. The same thing is true of your partner. If he or she is not pleasing you, remember that you've bought into that for now, so don't blame him or her either.

■ CREATE IT THE WAY YOU WANT IT
Fantasize freely about sex. If you discover you need more or better information than you now have, go get it. Plenty of good books are available. Form a picture in

your mind of just how you would like to feel about sex. Imagine yourself without guilt, able to ask for what you want. Don't get hung up in judging what you want. Write affirmations about loving your body and accepting your desires as natural. Remember, God gave us all instincts to be used unselfishly and constructively.

AFFIRMATIONS

1. I, _____, love my body and the pleasure it can give me.

2. I, _____, am willing to ask my partner to please me knowing that, as I am pleased, so will I please.

3. I, _____, deserve and enjoy sex as a natural part of my being.

16

HAVING MONEY IS YOUR RIGHT

Money is only a symbol of wealth and freedom and, in itself, possesses no magical powers other than the power men give it. But we give it all kinds of powers to avoid the responsibility of assuming these powers ourselves. We give money the power to make us secure, insecure, happy, miserable, healthy, ill, successful, sexy, beautiful, popular, powerful, weak, tense, relaxed, smart, dumb, better or worse than others—you name it—even immortal, through the money we leave our families.

In reality, money has none of these qualities or powers. Functionally, money is the medium of exchange that we use on this planet for the convenient and efficient trading of goods and services. Yet, through our fears and misperceptions, money has become one of the most misunderstood and complicated artifacts in our lives.

We have made a god of money and often treat money as though it had a mind of its own. Well, it doesn't. In fact, it does only what you tell it to do. It comes to you when you call it, and goes away when you reject it. The bottom line is that you create money through your own acceptance of your prosperity.

To understand what that means, it is first necessary to recognize that there are, in a sense, two worlds: one world without money and a second world with money. It's the world *without* money that creates the world *with* money. And the world *with* money can never create the world *without* money. The world without money is the world beyond the physical, the world in which we experience love, the appreciation of life and humanity, the real communication with one another. This is the spiritual world.

Of course, we live in a very real physical world, too, where our basic needs of food and shelter must be met. This physical world is God's gift to us, and the abundance and satisfactions are there for us to enjoy if we get our priorities right. The Bible explains these priorities: "Seek ye first the kingdom of God, and his righteousness; and all these things shall be added unto you" (Matthew 6:33).

The kingdom of God is the world without money, the world of love, sufficiency, and certainty. Unhappily, we have put the cart before the horse. We think that, if we have all these things added, money and all the physical things, we'll then experience the kingdom of God. We usually don't call it the kingdom of God but refer to it, instead, as "happiness." Because of our misorder of priorities, we think, "If I just had a little more money, I'd feel okay." If money is all that's needed, how do you account for all those people you see around you who have plenty of money but are still insecure and uneasy about life? No matter how people may try, they cannot make money a sufficient substitute for the spiritual life of fulfillment, satisfaction, and power.

You should remember each moment of your life that *spirit through mind creates the physical*. However, neither the spiritual nor the physical world has to prevail to the exclusion of the other, even though we often behave as though they were mutually exclusive. To illustrate what I mean, have you ever noticed that people often feel guilty not only about possessing money but about merely wanting money? This guilt stems from a sort of clouded awareness that they are trying to substitute the physical world for the spiritual world of fulfillment. And it is true that you can't make this substitution. *But you can have both.*

Job is a perfect example of what I'm talking about. Job started out complete, as we all do. He acquired material things and was prosperous and had a happy home. But Job began to feel guilty about his prosperity and happiness. He felt undeserving and unworthy and, in turn, proceeded to destroy everything he had. And things got worse and worse.

What had happened, of course, was that Job had changed his relationship to God, the source. The position of the source never changed. It never changes. The source is always affluent, abundant, and is total love and wisdom. But people, like Job, keep changing their relationship to the source. And it's the nature of that relationship that creates a particular physical world.

Thus, Job, through his fears and his acceptance of the negation of his life, lost his family, loved ones, and virtually all that he possessed. Fortunately, Job came to his senses and realized that the Father within was the source; and as he developed this awareness, he regained his family and wealth. In fact, he possessed more wealth than before. He was complete: he had everything.

The fact is that the Bible preaches prosperity, though somewhere along the line people got the notion that, if they experienced the prosperous—or moneyed—world, they were living in opposition to their true spiritual natures, in opposition to God. It's simply not so. But it is necessary to be aware that you live in both the spiritual and physical worlds. And it is necessary to be aware that, when you let your wealth and your money run you because you think that's what will give you what you want, you'll be destroyed. When you do that, you've made money a god.

Another feeling of discomfort suffered by people with money has to do with giving. Some are afraid to give, and others are afraid not to give. All of our relationships revolve around our willingness to give and receive. Receiving comes out of giving and the spirit in which we give. There are those who give out of fear, and that's not really giving. There are others who are afraid to give for fear they will lose what they have and there won't be any more left. And there are still others who think you have to give but you don't get anything back, so they give and don't receive.

Remember, the physical world comes out of our consciousness. As spiritual beings, we're complete, absolute, all-powerful, and all part of the omnipresent force. The spirit of each of us is the potential of form or experience. Through our mentality, concepts, beliefs, and attitudes, we as individuals direct the spirit potential into those concrete physical effects and forms we experience in life.

People find it difficult to believe that it is necessary to give first if they are to receive. But this is a universal law, and it applies to the gifts of love, attention, and respect just as it does to the gift of money. God is the source of abundance, and all kinds of material things are available to us. We can have as little or as much as we choose. But we must understand the spiritual laws.

One of these laws is the law of circulation. I recall a beautiful pond that was created on my grandmother's property when I was a child. The inflow to the pond came from a creek above, and the outflow went into another stream below. As long as there was this circulation of water, this pond was abundant with both plant and fish life. But in time, through neglect, both the inflow and outflow were cut off. Without circulation, this pond became stagnant and was no longer life supporting. Eventually, the pond died.

Well, love, respect, attention, and money, or prosperity, are exactly like the water in that pond: they must circulate, must flow in and out. Those people who hoard their love are takers, and takers are lonely people. And it's the same way with money. The universal law is that what you give, you get back. Give nothing, and you get nothing. Fail to abide by the spiritual law of circulation, and your relationships, personal or financial, become just as stagnant as that little pond. That is why we have tithing in the church; and that is why, when we don't tithe, our church loses its vitality and capacity for growth.

You must remain acutely aware that God is opulent and would not have put the bounty He has on this planet if you were not to enjoy it. To start creating what you want financially, you must use the law of the universe intelligently. That means accepting in your mind that God is the source and is abundant and that it's perfectly right for you to prosper, that you are not cheating God or anybody else by enjoying His magnificence—whether it's money, a work of art, a fine meal, a home, or whatever. And you must have the mental attitude that will allow you to experience this abundance.

Mental attitudes are incredibly important. Recently, I

counseled a young man who had been very successful financially. He had been divorced and had, as a part of the settle-
ment, given huge sums of money to his two children and his
wife. He had decided that money had ruined his marriage. He
vowed that money would never run him again, and he sought
God. But he noticed that, while he was trying very hard in the
financial world, he was no longer making any money.

In our counseling we discovered he felt that, if he were to
be prosperous now, his prosperity would ruin his new love
relationship, that money would once again become his god. I
pointed out to him that he was no longer the same man he
had been when he made the decision to divorce. He said: "Oh,
I didn't realize that. I'm not the same now, and money never
again will run my life. I accept that I absolutely deserve to
prosper." He realized that, with his new state of consciousness, money was a matter of personal choice. Yes, he wanted
money, but he realized that what kept him from prospering
was his decision seven years before that money and happiness
don't go together. Actually neither money nor happiness creates the other: happiness is a nonmoneyed experience and is
a function of accepting what's going on in your life. This man
is now able to accept both his happiness and his prosperity.
Money, he now knows, isn't good or bad: it just *is*.

As that example clearly indicates, we must give up our
reluctances about having money. But many myths and beliefs
about money block our receiving and create fear in giving.
Let's list a few of these common beliefs: Money is scarce. I
don't deserve it. I must be educated to be prosperous. Money
corrupts people. Money is evil. Money creates unhappiness
and infidelity in marriages. For me to be prosperous, somebody else must be deprived. I must be dishonest to get large

sums of money. The government will get all of my money, anyway. It's not God's will that I have money. If I work hard enough to make lots of money, I'll never have time for my family. I'll never have time for play. And on and on. There are few of us who don't, at one time or another, subscribe to a number of these beliefs. They have been passed down from generation to generation, and it is our acceptance of them that creates our unhappy relationship with money or our failure to have money.

For the people of the world to be prosperous, we must all accept our own divine inheritance and help and support others in accepting and having theirs. No one is better than another. We are all magnificent. Those who *have* bear an obligation to teach and assist others in *having*, and those who *don't have* have a responsibility to expand their prosperity consciousness and their willingness to make a contribution to the world.

Through objective observation of yourself and practice of the exercises at the end of this chapter, you will learn what powers you have given money and what barriers you have placed in the way of the universal law of abundance. You must determine how you wish to live and how to use the power of your imagination in the creation of goods and services, and you must accept the prosperity level that is rightfully yours. Merely wishing and hoping won't do it. You must be open to receive, be willing to enjoy, and look for opportunities to give. When you know who you are and where your source is, you'll have no fears about the success and prosperity of others and will be able to accept the prosperity level that is yours.

SELF-AWARENESS STRATEGIES
AND EXERCISES

▩ OBSERVE

Get in touch with your feelings about money. Watch how you handle your money. Do you wrinkle up your bills? How about your checkbook—is it balanced? How do you feel when bills arrive? Do you hesitate to open them?

Notice how you feel when you spend money. Do you feel that you are losing it or exchanging it?

What about asking for a raise?

▩ CHOOSE

Whatever your attitudes about money, whatever your current financial situation is, accept that you have chosen it. If your checkbook is not balanced, say, "I choose not to balance my checkbook." If you don't have enough money say, "I choose not to have enough money." Remember, you are setting the stage of your life for change.

▩ GIVE UP BLAME

Make whatever is going on in your life about money okay with you. If you are not earning enough, don't beat yourself up about it. Don't fall into the trap of making others wrong about your financial condition. Doing so simply puts the source outside you, and life doesn't work that way.

■ CREATE IT THE WAY YOU WANT IT

Decide just how you want your financial picture to be. Choose the amount of money you would like to have. Write a detailed description of the money you want and the way you want to handle it. Picture yourself depositing money into your bank accounts. See yourself withdrawing the money and spending it. See yourself comfortably paying your bills with the knowledge that you have a surplus. Imagine just how you will feel when you experience these things. Surround yourself with affirmations about your money so you will see and say them often, and with feeling.

AFFIRMATIONS

1. Everytime I, _____, give, I receive back my gift multiplied from sources known and unknown.

2. I, _____, love money and money loves me. With my money, I do good things for others, as well as for myself.

3. I, _____, know that my prosperity actually helps me be of service to myself and to others—my friends, family, loved ones, and even strangers.

17

THE MYTH OF COMPETITION

In many ways, the notion of competition is a myth. True, the appearance of all those people out there struggling among themselves for opportunity, money, status, and love suggests that competition is certainly going on. And most people believe that, to achieve, one must compete. Certainly, we all must work for what we want, but we don't have to compete, for competition is based on an erroneous interpretation of the nature of the universe. Those who compete do so out of a belief in lack and limitation, out of the belief that there's only a limited supply of good things out there. The fact is that there is total opportunity for each individual to fulfill his own dreams because the universe is filled with an ample supply of everything for everyone. Competition, really, is an ineffective form of rationing, for it occurs unnecessarily in a situation where the supplies are infinite. The myth of competition is that we think it is necessary.

We learn to compete at birth. We compete for attention, love, and nurturing. Competition is essentially a bid for attention; and as we grow older, we become junkies for attention. Much of our competition is the result of our addiction to parental approval and our belief that we must earn love. Here is where "what you think of me" runs my life.

Just look at the consequences: women compete with women; men compete with men; women compete with men, and men compete with women; mothers are jealous of daughters, and daughters are jealous of mothers; fathers and sons are jealous of one another—all part of the endless quest for attention and approval. We really want to love one another; but anger, jealousy, and competition intrude when we don't love ourselves and falsely look to another as the source. So, in a real sense, the only one you ever compete with is yourself. And, most important, when you see another as your source, it is easy to believe that there are just so many goodies out there.

When we see lack instead of abundance, we immediately create for ourselves a win-lose context. In perceiving that there is a limited supply of whatever it is that we want, we create the situation that, if we get some of it, someone else loses the portion we have gained. Or, conversely, if we don't get it, someone else does. We become concerned with who is getting the larger portions, we or they. These kinds of faulty concerns create much misery and unhappiness, and the kind of infighting we call "competition."

Ironically, life itself is a limitless resource. The source is infinite and never ending, and there is always more if you are willing to allow the Spirit to express itself fully through the creations of life. But when you believe in scarcity, you limit your own good. You create artificial limitations on yourself. The consequence of these limitations is often the need to beat the other person, to make sure that you don't lose, don't run out of things. Unfortunately, society reinforces this view with its beauty contests, races, and games that emphasize winning instead of participating or playing.

What most people fail to see is that, by being here on this planet, they have already won. Before conception, each one of us was a sperm and an egg. At the moment of conception, there was only one egg (or, occasionally, a few more in multiple births) and several million sperm. Each one of these sperm was a potential person. Just think for a moment! Of that potential several million, there is *you*! You will never again, as long as you live, undergo that kind of competition. You ran the incredible race for life, and you made it. You won! In this sense, the planet is full of winners. Each has won the right to play the game called life.

But most people play the game of life in such a way that all of their energies are focused on avoiding loss. They put their faith in others, look to people to create their happiness and good, depend on things outside themselves for fulfillment and satisfaction, and go to incredible lengths to protect their positions and to avoid what they regard as competition.

There are various ways of avoiding competition. One way is to try to eliminate the competitors. Some people try to stay ahead of everyone else. They work long hours, trying to earn more money. They sacrifice time that should be spent with their families.

In trying to eliminate competitors, they, of course, are competing. The phrase "keeping up with the Joneses" really means keeping ahead of them. Frequently, people feel that a bigger house, more cars, a food processor, and a microwave oven are evidence that they have won. Now there is absolutely nothing wrong with material wealth itself, but people who drive themselves to gain it at any cost are acting from the fear that, without it, they have lost. They fail to perceive that they have already won and that the purpose of life is to live it fully.

Another means people use of eliminating competitors is covertly undermining them. They gossip about others and stab them in the back. In the work setting, they are constantly maneuvering, by means of gossip and backbiting, to gain more power and control. We see similar actions in all areas of life. The woman who drives herself unmercifully to become president of the PTA, the man who whispers about the faults and weaknesses of others—all such people are acting out of the belief in lack. They are afraid to support others for fear that somehow they will lose when others gain. They simply don't see how it is possible for everyone to win. Their mistaken belief system is that, by putting down others, they will enhance their own position, a very typical misinterpretation of life made by those who come from lack and limitation.

Then, there are those who seek to avoid competition by simply giving up and refusing to play. We've all seen small children upset the Monopoly board and destroy the game rather than lose. Unfortunately, adults do the same thing. They think up all sorts of reasons and excuses for not playing. It's too expensive, they say. It's too difficult. It's too new, or others won't cooperate. At the bottom line, they are really saying: "I'm afraid I'll lose, so I won't play." They refuse to see the abundance in the universe and don't see how they could possibly win. They concentrate on not losing by not participating.

Whenever I feel a lack in my life, a sense that others are getting more than I am—whether it's love, nourishment, opportunity, money, appreciation, or respect—I have the opportunity to see that I haven't accepted these abundances for myself. When I see this, I can begin to take action. I can use these feelings to raise my consciousness and discover the things I really want in life.

You see, as I emphasize throughout this book, whatever you put your attention on persists. Jesus said: "What things soever ye desire, when ye pray, believe that ye receive *them*, and ye shall have *them*" (Mark 11:24). Ernest Holmes, who founded the Church of Religious Science over fifty years ago, said: "Every man must rely on his own consciousness, his immediate awareness of God, his authority in the law." When you speak your word, you are going to get a response from the universe. Whatever you put out there is absolutely what you are going to get back. If you continue to put your energy into competing with others to avoid loss, you will continue to lose. If you put your energy into stopping another, you are the one who will be stopped. When you concentrate on competing, you stop your own prosperity and creative expansion because you put aside your own individual goals and purposes.

The ironic fact is that often the people you are competing with don't even notice. They may be out there, getting where they want to go, doing what they want to do, experiencing love and full self-expression, because, consciously or unconsciously, they are using the creative law of the universe. Meanwhile, there you are, spending your energy, your life force, trying to win a game that no one else is playing.

How can you make competition work for you?

The first thing you must do to make competition work for you is stop fighting. In life, there is no need to stop to fight anything, because the universe is infinitely abundant, and there is more than enough for everyone. Every time you stop to fight, to compete, you simply stop yourself from going where you want to go. Remember, what you put your energy into persists.

The second thing you must do is reevaluate your own goals, purposes, dreams, and desires. When you discover that there is a person you want to compete with, treat this discovery as a signal to tell you what you really want. The fear that someone is getting where you want to go, or will take something away from you, becomes a valuable signpost, allowing you to clear up your intentions and goals, to determine what you *really* want so that you can get on with the important business of living.

What would happen if each and every one of us got clear on our intentions and put our energy into our own purposes and goals? Why, then, we would spend time clearing up our consciousness when it *wasn't* working for us and affirming our consciousness when it *was* working for us. We would take total responsibility for where we are and where we are going. We would let the power within create our desires for us. At that point, all of us would be absolutely satisfied, fulfilled, and prosperous.

But people get off the track. They set themselves up in win-lose situations—even no-win situations—because they are not clear on what they want. I know a man who persists in asking out women whom he knows will reject him. This constant rejection makes him feel that women are no good. And that's what he wants, because he is afraid of women. He keeps proving to himself that he is a loser. Now that's what competition can do: create inner fear and turmoil, feelings of inadequacy, the fierce striving that sets us up to feel that we are losers.

When we start to compete, it is out of this confusion, out

of the perception that whatever we want is scarce and that we are not complete. But each of us is complete; and when we really are conscious of our completeness, we can get beyond success and failure, get beyond judgment. When we become clear in our consciousness, we can participate in life and create the job, the event, and the style we want.

People get caught up in the form of what they want. Our current oil situation is an example. We don't have enough oil to supply our needs, yet we are surrounded by other energy sources. But we're caught up in the form, in the idea that only cars will get us around and that only oil can fuel cars. We become caught up in the idea of getting a certain job, rather than being conscious that a particular job is merely one form of the way we can create and be fulfilled. Or, we zero in on one person and, if that person doesn't like us, we become depressed, forgetting there are literally millions of other people out there.

Now it is true that, if you see every situation as a *race*, only one person can win it. But in that context, there are many situations and what often looks like losing is really a reflection of the individuality of people. It is a fact that no two people can ever occupy the same place at the same time because no two people have the same consciousness. And that which is yours is absolutely yours by right of consciousness. No one can take it away from you, and only you can destroy it.

So there are infinite numbers of races, and there is one to be won by each of us. There is a livelihood that is right for each of us, but we get confused. When we don't get the job we want, we become angry and feel we have lost rather than acquiring the consciousness to see that, perhaps, it simply was not the right job. We become unhappy when an important person in our life finds someone else, often overlooking that neither of us might have met the other's requirements.

What does work is to affirm the type of person and the kind of job you want, knowing that, if that particular person or job does not come your way, there is someone or something better still available to you. Once you accept in your consciousness that what you want in your life is an idea whose time has come, you will then allow the universal creative mind to bring these people and situations to you. Then, the people and the jobs will absolutely match you.

Finally, don't forget that you're already a winner just by being here on earth and that you have it all. Use your experience with competition to help you see what you truly want in life. Tell yourself the truth. Know that where you want to go and what you want to do are ideas whose time has come. Bless your competition for being an opportunity for insight. Then do what you need to do to get what you want. Make your life a win-win situation.

SELF-AWARENESS STRATEGIES AND EXERCISES

■ OBSERVE

How do you feel about competition? Do you feel you must compete, or that you always lose? Are there areas in your life where you feel you must win?

How do you feel when it looks like you've lost something—a game, a job, an election? How do you feel about the person who won?

Notice if you truly believe that there is an ample supply for everyone. Or do you feel the universe is limited?

■ CHOOSE

Choose your feelings, your actions. Make them yours, and make them okay by knowing that you choose them. If you feel very competitive, say, "I choose to feel very competitive—that I have to win." If you feel that you are a loser, choose that. The more you accept that you are responsible, the more you are willing to choose what you now have, the more able you will be to create what you want.

■ GIVE UP BLAME

Don't put yourself down for your feelings or your actions. Don't allow yourself to feel guilty or stupid. God does not make junk, and you can use these experiences to learn. Don't try to lay the blame on anyone else either. The only way you can be suppressed is if you allow it.

■ CREATE IT THE WAY YOU WANT IT

Visualize just how you would like to be and feel in seemingly competitive situations. If you compete with members of the same or the opposite sex, imagine how you would like to behave. What would you say? What would you do? What would they do and say? Get a clear picture of the way you want it to be. Write affirmations and place them where you will see them often.

AFFIRMATIONS

1. I, _____, know that there is an ample supply of everything for everybody.

2. I, _____, support myself and others in finding their right job, mate, home, and so forth.

3. I, _____, know that I am a winner, and I support everyone around me in winning, too.

18

THE POWER OF
MAKING A DECISION

Decisions become easy when you give up the need for approval and the fear of making mistakes. There are all kinds of decisions, big ones and little ones. The big ones are usually those that involve an either-or situation; the little ones are usually the day-to-day choices that confront us, choices where the options may be numerous. Both kinds cause unnecessary trouble.

The narrow choice, the either-or, involved in big decisions terrifies some people. Similarly, other people suffer anxiety when confronted with the numerous options that usually accompany small decisions. In both instances, people are driven crazy by the need to be "right," which usually translates into: "What do others expect of me?"

It may come as a surprise to you that the decisions that foul up the most people are the day-to-day decisions. I find in my counseling that some people are immobilized by what others regard as the mere mechanics of daily living: Should I make a phone call or not? Should I order the newspaper or not? Should I get out of bed? Should I wash my hair? And on and on. Some people get stuck on these decisions. Each one becomes monumental. And any one can literally tie up their entire day.

Ironically, I find that people responsible for so-called big decisions, people running large organizations, who make decisions affecting the lives of large numbers of people, make decisions more easily than those confronted only with the day-to-day mechanics of living. My own experience is that the more decisions I make, the more effortless decision making becomes. As I make bigger decisions, it becomes easier to make other decisions. Conversely, I find that when I make fewer decisions in my life, I assume less responsibility for myself and the world around me. Then the piddling, everyday kinds of decisions become monumental and control me.

Avoidance of big or little decisions involves the same kinds of inner feelings. The biggest reason for indecision is fear of not making the "right" decision. This fear is characteristic of people who have a limited purpose in life. Let me illustrate. Look at those people with an expanded purpose. Their purpose may be to clean up the environment or to transform other people's lives. Maybe they want to see that all children are treated with respect, or that pets are neutered and given good homes. Perhaps their purpose is to grow the most magnificent radish in the world. Whatever it is, their purpose is larger than they are, larger than their job, larger than the immediate things going on in their lives.

When you have such an expanded purpose, you will find that many decisions, which at first seemed monumental, become small in comparison with your goal. When your purpose in life is large, your office is no longer your entire world. Your relationship with one person is not your entire life. In this context, the failure to make the "right" decision in any given instance is not the end of the world. The significance of any one decision is lessened. You can see that there are all sorts of other opportunities, and that a faulty decision is simply a mistake, a learning experience, one you don't have to repeat. You just do your best and get on with it.

In addition to the preoccupation with making the "right" decision, another immobilizer is the belief that there is no solution. People can get so caught up in the problem that they can't see the way out. This belief, in turn, leads to the belief that you must compromise. I find often that people get so involved in compromise that they compromise their lives away. I personally don't even like the word "compromise" because it automatically implies that someone's going to lose. We seem to feel that, if we both lose a little, it's all right: I won't feel too bad because you lost, too. When we're clear in our purpose and willing to make decisions, everyone can win. When you move to compromise in a decision, you've already given up on the idea that you can have what you want. You've given up on your power. You're trying to make a decision through the avoidance of loss, and that's like trying to say yes when you want to say no. Everyone loses.

Inevitably, the problem of decisions gets back to the question of, "What do I really want?" Most people can think only of immediate goals. But if you broaden your perspective on life and expand your view and your purpose, you can see that you are greater than what you are involved in right now. Then decisions are not so scary, and there is not as much at stake. Of course, there never really is that much at stake, except in our imaginations.

But you must have a well-defined greater purpose in your life. Then, you can see whether the decisions you are making are moving you toward the fulfillment of that purpose, or moving you away from it. Does the decision support you in your aim, or does it suppress you? That's not difficult to determine if you are clear about your greater purpose. And that easy determination makes the decision itself easy.

The reason having a greater purpose eases the burden of decision making is that it provides a criterion, a measure, that can be objectively applied to any situation. We can assess our decisions on the basis of whether they advance or suppress our purpose. Life, then, becomes more than just a game of chance: it requires skill and strategy. But decision making becomes easy.

Unfortunately, we try to make life a mystery. It's not life that is mysterious, but ourselves. As we begin to confront ourselves and become willing to say what we want to say, to go where we want to go, to do what we want to do, then the mystery in ourselves clears up. The biggest mysteries are created by the lies we tell ourselves. It is difficult to be honest with ourselves because we're programmed to feel that others won't approve. Actually, the reverse is true. The more we tell ourselves the truth, then act on that honesty, the more effective we become. When we lie to ourselves, we destroy the guidelines that tell us what's supportive and what's not supportive of our purpose. Then, when a decision confronts us, it becomes a hit-or-miss proposition.

We make so many decisions for the wrong reasons. These reasons are all tangled up in our fears. We fear we'll make the "wrong" decision, the decision that meets with disapproval. Or, in rebellion against an authority figure, we intentionally make a decision we *know* will be disapproved of. We tell ourselves that we are asserting our independence, that we are not letting that authority figure influence us. Yet all the while we are making a decision "at" that person, if not "for" that person. We are not doing what we want but are, instead, doing what someone else *doesn't* want. Our decisions, then, become nothing more than a way to get even with those who have imposed their demands upon us.

We often think: "Well, I live my own life, make my own decisions and choices." Yet when we examine these decisions and choices, we note they all have something in common: they are all in opposition to someone else—mothers, fathers, mates, and so on. Decisions in opposition to someone else are no more satisfactory than decisions made to conform to the desires of someone else. If we are caught between the decision approaches of opposition and the decision approaches of conformity, then we are immobilized.

Decision fears, of course, are compounded by the notion that, if I step outside my bounds, I'll destroy the relationship, I'll lose, be abandoned and rejected. When we give up our right to make decisions in hope that a relationship will continue, we give up the right to be who we are. The usual result is that the relationship deteriorates in direct proportion to how much of ourselves we give up. On the other hand, if we are true to ourselves and decide what we want and ask for it, a magnificent relationship is possible.

Another big decision fear is that, if you make this decision and it's successful, you'll have to go on to the next step. This is another immobilizer. If you don't move, you don't have to handle more responsibility in your life, you don't have to handle more success, you don't have to handle more money. In such a situation, you are making decisions by default, and you are abdicating your life.

Then, there's the fear that, if you make the decision, you'll look like a fool. This is closely allied with the need to be "right" all the time. This fear is based on the sneaking suspicion that you are not okay and, perhaps, should quit trying to prove that you are. "Maybe," you tell yourself, "if I just quit trying, I'll discover that I am okay." Again, you abdicate your life, thereby proving to yourself once again that you were right all along: you're not okay. This becomes a vicious circle of lies, because you are a wonderful spiritual being, a capable, loving, and magnificent creature of God.

Another curious block to decision making is the fear that other people will lose because of your decision. In such a situation, you think your decision might "hurt" the seemingly helpless partner, and that, if you win, he or she loses. As you contemplate your decision, you say, "I'll hurt him," or "I'm really selfish if I do this." Well, in my counseling, I find that most people, deep down in their hearts, are not trying to hurt others. They hurt out of a sense of self-preservation or in an attempt to keep from being hurt: "I'll get you first before you get me." When you've raised your consciousness, you can see that this assumption is not so, that the fear of hurting another is unfounded, because we are in a win-win situation: no one is "hurt"; no one loses.

If your decisions are about expanding self-awareness, if your decisions are about more life, more self-expression, more love, then you will find that they are the right decisions. If you want for others the happiness and love and abundance you want for yourself, if you really want them to be all they choose to be, and your decision doesn't run counter to that, then it's a good decision. If, on the other hand, you observe that your decision is going to rip people off in some way, it's a useless decision because it won't work. You get back what you give out.

Then, there are certain kinds of decisions that intimidate us simply because we don't have the information required to make them. Take an investment situation. Many people, aware that they don't know much about real estate, the stock market, or investing, simply turn the matter over to someone else. That's not responsible. And if things turn out wrong, they say they were cheated. Actually, they refused to acquire the needed information. In decisions such as these, you have a responsibility to determine what you want and what kinds of information and new skills are necessary for you to decide intelligently.

Considering all of the decisions that confront us, the little ones and the big ones, how do we learn to make responsible decisions?

First, make your decisions based very specifically on what you want. Be willing to trust your intuition. Intuition is that feeling inside that tells you whether you're on the right path or not. We all have intuition and can and should learn to listen to it. Intuition is quite different from thought. Thought, if not based on our enlarged sense of purpose, can deteriorate into worthless worrying and lead us into immobility. You can train your intuition by using it and observing the results. When you get results you don't want, you probably have not been telling yourself the truth about what you do want.

In confronting a decision, ask yourself if all the fears you have weren't realized, if you knew whatever decision you made would really work out, which choice would you make? If everything were ideal, what would you choose? Clear away the need for approval, the fear of "hurting" others, and the fear of loss and failure. Assume these considerations don't exist. Now, what decision will you make? What alternative will you choose?

Apply this method in making your decisions. Perhaps you should practice first with small decisions, the day-to-day ones that immobilize so many people. As you begin making small decisions, you will discover that you can move on comfortably to larger ones. You'll soon see that the decisions that were difficult last month are easier now.

You don't become less fearful by avoiding decisions. On the contrary, inaction makes you more fearful. Because you make no decisions, you think there are no solutions. You find no way out. You forget that, because you found a way *in*, you can certainly find a way *out*.

I used to keep a sign in my office that said: "Pray to God, but row to shore." That means you need to back your prayers up with real personal effort. When you do your self-awareness exercises and make your affirmations, you also need to act. You have to confront your circumstances and *make* your decisions.

SELF-AWARENESS STRATEGIES AND EXERCISES

■ OBSERVE

Notice those times when you don't want to make a decision. What are you feeling? What are the fears that come up for you? Are you afraid you will look like a fool if you don't make the "right" decision?

What about the decisions you have been postponing? Notice how the pressure has been building. Look to see if you tend to repeat this type of pattern over and over again.

Notice how you feel around people who are indecisive. How do you feel about people who make decisions without hesitation?

Look at the decisions you have made in the past. How do you feel about them? Make a list of the decisions you have felt good about.

■ CHOOSE

Decide now to take responsibility for your life. If you don't like making decisions, say, "I choose not to make decisions." If decision making makes you afraid, say, "I choose to be afraid of making decisions." Whatever your situation is, choose it and make it okay for you now.

■ GIVE UP BLAME

If you're uncomfortable with decisions, just accept that fact. Don't make yourself wrong over it. If you have blamed other people for keeping you from making decisions, stop blaming now. You are in control of your own life, and people and places and things can't confuse you unless you let them.

■ CREATE IT THE WAY YOU WANT IT

Look again at the list of good decisions you have made. Remember how good you felt when you made the decision, how pleased you were with the result. Look at the decisions you are facing now. Get clear on the result you want. Look at your larger purpose. Visualize how you will feel when you have the result you want. Get started now making decisions—small ones, large ones. Start practicing now.

AFFIRMATIONS

1. I, _____, am comfortable making decisions and am confident about the results.

2. I, _____, know that my decisions are for the highest good and are in the best interest of all concerned.

3. I, _____, accept and enjoy the challenge of the decisions I make in my life knowing that I choose wisely because I listen to my inner voice.

19

ARGUE FOR YOUR LIMITATIONS AND THEY ARE YOURS

"To fly as fast as thought, to anywhere that is,"
he said, "you must begin by knowing that you have
already arrived . . ."

The words of Chiang, an older gull, as quoted by
Richard Bach in *Jonathan Livingston Seagull*

That quote from *Jonathan Livingston Seagull* inspires me and touches that part of me that knows I can be, do, and have what I want in my life, that part of me that knows no limitations. But there is another part of me (it exists in all of us) that buys into the limitations that humankind has accepted. That's the part of me (and you), the conditioned mind, that is the storehouse of my beliefs and interpretations of every experience I have ever had. I only feel trapped by my circumstances when I forget that I am the one who creates my environment, when I let the mental tape recordings of yesterday run my life.

We have the power over the physical world to create during each moment of our lives. Unhappily, we are taught the reverse: that what we have determines what we do which, in turn, creates who we are.

To illustrate what I mean, take the expression "seeing is believing." That means you believe in something when you can see it. But there are others who can see beyond what already exists, who have the vision to see beyond appearances. Such people know that what exists now was once an idea. I look at the building where my office is. I know there was a time when it did not exist. First, the owner of the land had the idea to create a building. He called in an architect and explained what he wanted in terms of size, appearance, and function. The architect, consulting with the owner, drew up plans, a blueprint. A contractor took the plans and, with his workmen, built the building. Thus, the owner's *idea*, through the *doing* of owner, architect, contractor, and workmen, produced the *having* of a building.

There is only one rule for creation. It's the same one, whether applied to buildings, relationships, health, boats, cars—you name it. That rule is that my idea creates my behavior, which creates results. The confusion occurs when people begin looking for a different creative rule to apply to each of the various areas of their life. But there is only one rule. My idea—call it notion, concept, or attitude, if you wish—creates the manner in which I handle myself in all situations. And how I handle myself determines the results I achieve.

What happens has nothing to do with physical forms, whether we are talking about buildings, bodies, or cars. The idea is the beginning: it creates the action or behavior. The action or behavior determines the results. That is the system you must use to create anything in your life.

Just where do you start? Well, you have to start with what you want. Sounds simple, but people have more trouble in determining what they want than you would think.

For example, when troubled people come to me for counseling, I find they want to tell me their life history. "So you will understand where I am," they explain. My reply is: "I'm not interested in your past or what was. What I want to know is what do you want to do now." It's amazing how few of them actually stay on course and say "what I want is this." They'll generalize and meander all over the place. I explain to them that they have to state *exactly* what they want. Otherwise, there is no blueprint for a specific result.

To return to the analogy of how my office building was created, you are, in effect, the owner, architect, contractor, and workmen. You have to know *exactly* the end result you want if you are to create the blueprint that will lead to the construction of the reality. A certain timidity prevents many of us from stating *exactly* what we want. At the time, it may seem unrealistic, and we fear that others will think we are foolish. In fact, your skills may be less than what are needed to achieve the goal you seek. Nevertheless, you have to say what you want, even if it appears unrealistic, unreasonable, unattainable.

Why is it necessary to say *exactly* what you want? It is necessary because, if you allow the conditions of your life now to determine what you are going to create in the future, then you are constantly trapped by the limitations of the past. You are continually caught in the conditioning, the attitudes, and the beliefs that you agreed upon, consciously or unconsciously, in the past. What's going on in your life right now is the end result of the ideas you accepted before now. In other words, whatever is going on now, you set it up previously. To create what you really want in the future, you've got to transcend the trap of those prior decisions and beliefs.

I find there are three circumstances that usually stand in the way of creating what you say you want. The first of these, and possibly the most important, is that you haven't taken your idea far enough. You stopped short. As an illustration, let's take an experience of mine.

For years I had wanted to do a television program. I knew I had the ability, even though at that time it was not evident. Though the program seemed far from where I was at the time, I knew in my heart it was what I wanted to do. So, my affirmation was "I have my own television show." Not "I want to have a television show," but "I *have* my own television show." There's an important difference that I will explain later.

Well, from my affirmation, people came along and helped me to do a television show. It was called *The Terry Cole Show*, and a Los Angeles company actually paid for it. I did one show on tape, and it was simply awful, terrible. I was embarrassed, humiliated. Naturally, the station did not put it on the air. So I bought the tape and kept it.

Three years passed, and I was still saying I wanted my own television show. I couldn't figure out why things weren't working. There is only one rule, I reminded myself: ideas are created into form. So if I don't have the results I want, it must be that I don't have the right idea. I got out my old papers where I had written my affirmations. It was important to see *exactly* what I had written. The words, themselves, are important because they set up the context in which you create. As I reread these old affirmations, I discovered they said it was my goal to have my own television show. Suddenly the light flashed on. I *did have* it—out in the garage in a can. I had my own tape. What I really wanted was to *do* my own successful weekly television show that transformed people's lives, a show that was successful in all areas, financially abundant, and worldwide. That affirmation set up a whole new context; and within two weeks I was into production of my weekly, successful television program, *The Terry Cole-Whittaker Show.*

There are still things that need to be handled from time to time; and in doing the show, I can see where my barriers are and where they aren't. In creating the life you want, you argue in favor of your abilities and your power to do what's working. If it isn't working, let go of it. Don't do it. You must constantly check the physical realities, because the results you get don't lie. The results will tell you what idea you really have about the particular situation.

So, the first principle again: you must take your idea far enough. If you say, "I want to clean out the garage," you probably won't get any further than started. What you want to do is affirm: "I have completed cleaning my garage, and it is neat and orderly." Instead of saying, "I want to meet my right mate," you affirm, "I am with my right mate and we enjoy and love one another." Whatever you want, take it far enough. And if you want to know how far your ideas take you, simply look at what you have. That will tell you. If you are satisfied, great. If not, sit down and determine what you really want.

A second circumstance that often stands in the way of creating what you say you want is the interference of someone else's idea. The goals you wish to create can't be your mother's idea, your father's, your husband's, your wife's, your kid's, or anyone else's. They have to be *your* idea. Unfortunately, in choosing the goals to create, we often don't really know what we want in our hearts. So, we accept as our own the goals of others, not only the goals of others who are close to us but the goals suggested by TV commercials and magazine ads. As a consequence, it is important to examine what you say you want. You may discover that you don't even want it, but are committed to it because someone else has recommended it as a goal for you.

The third circumstance that may block your achievement of what you want involves limitations. Now there are some real limitations. Jumping out of a plane without a parachute and affirming that "I'll land safely" is most likely to prove that gravitational attraction is a very real limitation. But most limitations are not real. Or, if they are, there may be ways around them. You may love the idea of staying underwater for a long time, but there is the real limitation that your body requires a continuous supply of oxygen, which your lungs cannot extract from the water. You get around this limitation by carrying your oxygen supply with you. Gravity is definitely a limitation, determining how high you can jump. Yet, by understanding gravity, men were able to build machines that could break away from this planet and land on the moon. So, even most of the so-called *real* limitations are not necessarily obstacles when they are understood. You should keep that in mind when you observe what seem to be real challenges to your achievement of what you want.

But most of the obstacles are unreal, simply limitations you've allowed your mind to accept. Remember, the Bible warns about judging on the basis of appearances. Remember, also, that appearances are essentially creations of yesterday. If you are to create what you want, you disregard appearances and start from scratch. For when we create in the highest sense, we do so from the Spirit, which has nothing to do with what already is. We create from nothing in the physical sense. Yet, most people dissipate their creative energies, trying to avoid, resist, change, or destroy what already exists, what they already have. In trying to design a new house—or a new life—they try to alter or remodel what they already have. Appearances and limitations make us think we are locked into what we already have, that we are stuck there.

Real creation comes out of your mind unobstructed, starting with a whole new concept, a whole new blueprint. Your subconscious is a creator, a problem solver. The solutions to your problems come out of your willingness to have the problem solved and to know the result you want. The funny thing is that we are always creating, either problems or solutions.

But, always, we come back to determining, honestly, what you want. One way of starting is by listing, on the left side of a page of paper, your dissatisfactions. In the middle of the page, write what you want, and on the right-hand side, write down what you need to do to get what you want. That, at least, will tell you what action to take. Whatever the step, you will be surprised that once you get your mind going in the area of solutions, the solutions start appearing.

Unfortunately, so much of our energy goes into coping with and worrying about our problems that we are left powerless to be, do, and have what we want in life. If you think you can't create what you want, take a look at what you've got. Then take a look at what you believe about what you've got. Look at all the energy you are using to keep things the way they are. Notice that you are arguing in favor of your limitations. You are arguing in favor of the problem, in favor of no solution, and in favor of those three ideas that drive people crazy: I can't get out of this situation; if it's good, it's not going to last; and there's just barely enough out there for me and all the others. Those basic ideas proliferate into all kinds of other excuses, such as "I don't have the time," "it's unrealistic," and on and on.

We all think our problems are different. I find in counseling that, invariably, people argue that their problem is unsolvable. They argue about how limited they are and that there's no way out. There's little doubt that they want a way out, but usually they are afraid of the way out. They are trapped in their beliefs.

It is important that we all challenge constantly the ideas that come into our minds. As we do this, we discover that we are surrounded by relatives, friends, strangers, the media—all of whom are passing on their belief systems. We are all suckers for advice. You will discover that, when you take advice from people, your life usually comes to resemble theirs. How many people take advice about child-rearing from people whose own children are a mess? You can *learn* from others, but don't take *advice* from them. If you want to know how to get where you want to go, go talk to someone who is *really* there already. If you talk to him, he'll tell you how he got there. In doing so, he is not *advising* you but describing what he has done. You will discover there is a system he followed; and that system demanded that first, he had to know what he wanted, and second, he had to acknowledge that, in a sense, he was already there.

Always standing in the way are what I call the "but" beliefs: "I could do it *but* I can't wait that long . . . *but* I don't have enough money . . . *but* I don't know how." You have to get rid of the "buts," because if you argue for your limitations long enough, sure enough, they are yours. Start arguing in favor of what you want and recognize that *persistence* is the key.

Many years ago someone said something to me that became indelibly impressed on my mind: "Terry, if you just keep at what you are doing long enough, you will naturally rise to the top because the great majority of the people, through the simple law of averages, will drop away." I'm not proposing you settle for that ineffective kind of success, but I make the reference simply to emphasize that persistence is a critical value for all of us.

Again, I repeat, *determine exactly what you want and accept the idea that you are already there.* One technique for accepting that you are already there is the *affirmation.* Now some people find it tough to accept the affirmations. They ask: "How can I say 'I am well' when I am sick?" I explain that sickness is faulty problem solving (see Chapter 7) that arises out of dependency and fear of confronting our problems.

In making an affirmation, what you do is set up the context within which what you want can happen. In writing an affirmation, you use the first person, "I," then state your name, and very specifically state positively what you want and in the present tense. For example, "I, Terry, love to exercise daily and it is fun." That's an affirmation. You might think, "Well, I know I should exercise, but I hate it." Fine, that's a belief. Then, go through the action of exercising, and make a decision. You either liked it or you didn't. It was tiring, boring, or it was fun, and so on. You will have demonstrated to you that your belief—fun or boring—will be validated. Once you get the idea of this validating of your beliefs, you can start drawing from the limitless reservoir of your mind. If exercising is no fun, you choose an exercise that is fun. You continue to make your affirmations, give them more thought, advance the idea, such as: "My body is firm, strong. I enjoy exercising. It is fun. I feel a tremendous amount of energy." You can apply these affirmations to any situation in your life, and as I said earlier, you are setting up the context in which you allow the new situation to take place.

Now, I don't know how it's going to take place or who is going to come into your life to do it. In being reasonable, we think that, once we know what we want, we have to figure out right now how it's going to happen. Well, you can think about it, but doing so is not going to give you the answer. Your responsibility is to take the action indicated by your goal and affirmation. Your subconscious creative machine will take over and become the problem solver. All kinds of things will happen, but they will happen within the context that you already have it.

Now, if that seems confusing, just think about it this way. In a sense, it's like being ready when an opportunity comes along. Obviously, you can't have what you don't know that you want. But if you determine what you want and ask for it, you may discover that the element that will bring it about was already there. Your affirmations are a means of changing not only your beliefs but also your perceptions. So, relax and write down or record your affirmations. Accept what you want and accept that you already have it.

Stick with your affirmations, even though appearances may say differently, for appearances will change. Learn from every experience you have, and use each one to your advantage. Really, your life is a great adventure, and you can create it the way you want it. You've been doing that already, but most likely unconsciously. Bring up the level of your consciousness and watch the miracles take place in your life.

SELF-AWARENESS STRATEGIES
AND EXERCISES

■ OBSERVE

Observe the way your life is now. See if you can find the patterns that brought you to this place. Notice those things you like about your life and those things you want to change.

Make a list of the problems you have, and beside each problem, list the way you would like it to turn out, to be. Notice what comes up for you when you do this. Do you feel fear? Do you feel your goals are impossible? Do you become angry?

■ CHOOSE

Accept the fact that you have created your life to this point. You know how your life is going to turn out. Right at this moment your whole life has been about getting to the place where you could sit down and read this sentence. This is it. Become comfortable with this thought. Laugh at it if you can.

■ GIVE UP BLAME

If you feel you've been wrong, get off your own back. Quit beating yourself up. Don't fall into the trap of blaming others for your current situation. Remember, whatever number might have been run on you, you agreed to play.

■ CREATE IT THE WAY YOU WANT IT

Go back to your list of problems and the solutions you want. Beside each goal write the steps you think you will need to take to get there. Don't be afraid to be outrageous. Now create an affirmation for each situation. For instance, if you've written down that your problem is not enough money and that your solution is more money and the steps are to get the skills to earn more money, write, "I, _____, now have the job that pays me $_____ per month." Be specific about the amount of money. Now visualize just what it will be like for you to have that job and that amount of money. Picture yourself receiving your new paycheck. See yourself depositing it in the bank. Imagine yourself writing the checks to pay your bills. Feel how it will be when you have enough money.

Make a treasure map for yourself. Find pictures of the things you want, pictures that represent the way you want your life to be. Paste these pictures on a large piece of poster board and write a short, one-line affirmation under each one. Hang this map where you will see it several times a day. You can have one at home and another at the office. Take a moment or two several times each day to look at your map and to repeat your affirmations. You can also paste or tape one-line affirmations to the mirror in your bathroom, the dashboard of your car, the top of your desk—anywhere where you will see them frequently.

AFFIRMATIONS

1. I, _____, know what I want and am using affirmation to change my life for the better now.

2. I, _____, accept that I have everything and everyone I want in my life now and that my happiness enhances other people.

3. I, _____, have a creative mind and create my world to suit me now.

20

WHAT YOU THINK OF ME IS NONE OF MY BUSINESS

Whatever the nature of the specific problems we have discussed in this book, I think you will see that virtually all of our problems are either caused or compounded by our obsessive need for acceptance and approval from other people. This need—a false one, I might add—permeates all areas of our lives, our relationships at home and work, how we spend our money, the way we dress, the way we respond to both loved ones and strangers. It even affects the kind of food we eat and what time we get up in the morning. This need to please other people causes us to have lifestyles that are not satisfying and to remain in relationships that are not supportive. Carried to the extreme—and it often is—this need to please others can cause illness, poverty, and even death.

You see, if I run my life on the basis of what you think of me, I destroy my own self, my essence, even the God within that can allow me to be loving, healthy, abundant, and fully self-expressed. To the degree that I live my life in an effort to please others, I chip away at myself. If I focus my energies on pleasing other people, my life will be less magnificent than it can be. If, in the effort to please, I allow others' ideas to control everything I do, my life will be one of constant confusion and dissatisfaction.

When I say, "What you think of me is none of my business," I am not saying, "I don't listen to what is said." If I refused to listen, I would actually close the door on the opportunity to have learning experiences. What I mean is that, *ideally*, I can use what you think of me as a guide and a mirror for my own life. The reflection of myself in what you say about me *can* give me a clearer view of myself and allow me to grow as a person. But more often, I use this reflection—or input from others—to make myself feel guilty, wrong, and insecure. I then try to change my act to please others, and the vicious circle begins. In that sense, what you think of me *should be* none of my business.

Each time another expresses an opinion about me, I have two choices: I can either take the view of another and use it to reinforce negative mental patterns I already have, or I can use the information to get rid of that which I do not want. If I choose the latter, I have the opportunity to grow, to improve, in any area of my life—my job, my relationships, my health.

You see, to the degree that we can take a really good look at ourselves and see ourselves objectively and lovingly, we are able to participate more fully in this life. Most of us can see ourselves to a certain degree, but often our objective and loving view of ourselves is very narrow, particularly if we rely on others for confirmation of how we see ourselves.

It is absolutely imperative that each of us learns to love himself or herself, and that's what this book is about. When I say, "Love yourself," I'm not talking about an ego trip or indulgence in pride. I'm talking about the universal truth that each of us is an individualized expression of God. And God doesn't make junk. It is only out of this objective self-love that we are able to love our neighbors, to tell the truth about what we want, and to experience life at its fullest.

Unfortunately, too often we look to other people to give us what we think we need and waste a lot of time trying to get what we want from them. We become self-obsessed, and the result is that we never feel really okay about ourselves. We judge ourselves constantly, and our verdict is usually guilty.

In fact, our relationships with other people provide a tremendous opportunity. If we are open to feedback from people, we can learn great truths about ourselves. But being open to feedback is completely different from plugging into others for our good. We plug in when we hunger and thirst for their approval. But when we love ourselves and are able to be sincere with ourselves, we can look at what others say and decide, objectively, if it has any value or truth in it for us. This objective opening up releases our own potential and our ability to participate more fully in every area of life. Being objective, of course, is not easy, but we can learn.

Now there is a great difference between taking an objective view of what others think of us and allowing them to dump their own insecurities and fears upon us. Certainly, people can and need to express themselves to you, but you don't have to agree. Unhappily, we tend to plug into their hang-ups and their ideas of how life and our behavior should be. Sure, everyone has a point of view, doubts and expectations, and that's all it is—*theirs*. We tend to take it personally, to make it *ours*, and to feel the need to defend and make excuses. In doing so, we lose our objectivity. Just remember that, when others seek to dump their insecurities on you, what they are really saying is simply a reflection of where *they* are.

One of the basic principles of life is stated in Matthew 8:13: "Go thy way; and as thou hast believed, *so* be it done unto thee." That simply means that your beliefs create your personal reality. You are made in the image and likeness of God and, as such, are already perfect. If each of us could truly accept that fact in all areas of our life right now, we would experience the Christ consciousness. We would totally love ourselves, totally love everybody else; and no matter what we were involved in, we would accept ourselves, and our lives would be magnificent adventures. The principle is simple, but at times it isn't easy to apply.

What we are talking about, essentially, is reloving ourselves, reestablishing the conscious contact with the universal power. You aren't learning to love yourself: you're relearning it. You are remembering it, remembering that each person comes from God and is, therefore, good. But we forget that fact and mislead ourselves into all kinds of confused and harmful behaviors.

Let's look at a person and see what really goes on. You may use yourself as an example; for really, we are all alike, and once you understand *you*, you will understand others. So we start with a typical day, waking up and getting out of bed. Along with putting on your clothes, you also put on the person you are every morning. You put on your personality, your act for the day. You then go out and play your role in life.

The role people usually play is created by the way others have responded and reacted to them. Beneath that role is the real self, but we are afraid to let that real self out for fear that it might be evil or bad, or that it won't fit or match up. That's the reason we go through life trying to behave the way we think we should, rather than the way we want to.

This process starts a long way back—at birth, in fact, and possibly even before. When we are born, we are dependent on our parents. We learn quickly that the way to get attention is to cry. How many of us were picked up and loved because we were clean, happy, and quiet? From the very beginning, we learn to gain attention, which is a form of approval, when something goes wrong. Because we genuinely need things like food and shelter, we learn to associate getting what we need from our parents with gaining their approval.

It's not hard to see how we become attached to other people's opinions of us. Unless we grew up in an exceptionally supportive environment, we are apt to think, deep down, that we are really no good. Think about the child who really wants to stay at a party and the mother who says: "Okay, you can stay, but I'm leaving and then how'll you get home?" Now this might work for a teenager who has learned how to take a bus or get a ride with someone else; but for the small child, this can be a traumatic experience. To the child, the experience means abandonment; and he has no idea what he's done to deserve it. Whatever it was, it was wrong. It must have been! Or, so the child thinks.

All the child wanted to do was stay at the party. Somehow he has made himself wrong and quickly learns to be very careful or else face abandonment. And it's not a big jump from this to feeling that somehow he is bad. What the child has done is to take somebody else's action, misinterpret that person's opinion, and make this distorted perception his own. Because he's convinced he's bad, wrong, he literally *needs* the approval of others to make him good, right.

From misinterpretations of similar experiences, we learn

to run our lives and get what we want. From these experiences, we create our views of ourselves. Is it any wonder, then, that it's hard to grow up without being suppressed? If our parents don't do it, schools and playmates will. We are told so often not to do certain things because of "what people will think" that we are overcome with the feeling that we must please others to survive. And in this need to please others, we stifle our true selves. This denial of our true selves becomes so strong that eventually we don't even know what we really want. Thus, we spend lifetimes suppressing our own desires because we think we have to get along with people to survive.

Let's take a look at the real self. Your real self, as other parts of this book have emphasized, is totally perfect, complete, loving, and powerful. The real self does not have to get what it needs from anyone else: others are not the source. But our insidious memories remind us that we were once small and vulnerable and needed the help of big people to survive. So, we build whole lifestyles on what we think they wanted from us. In many instances, the price of adulthood has been very high, for we have given up our very real and powerful essence.

Put simply, the time has come to stop basing your self-image on what others think. Every time you allow your life to be run by others' wishes, you give up some more of yourself. Just think of a few familiar examples. You might want to quit your job, but you're afraid people will think you are lazy or a malcontent. You may stay married to a nonsupportive spouse because you fear the disapproval of friends and relatives. Or, you may make your kids conform to other people's standards, merely for the sake of appearance. And long after you have left your childhood home, you may still be running your life based completely on what your parents (even after they're dead) would think. Remember that *you* are responsible for *your own* life. What you believe is the way it's going to be.

There is another way to look at life, a way that may give you the courage to ask for what you want. In many ways, we come into the world alone, even though we may be a twin or born into a large family. We live alone and die alone. This is a paradox because we are surrounded by people, and at the spiritual core we are all one. But because we can only feel what we feel and do what we do, we are, in various ways, alone. There is no way another can live your life; nor can you live the life of another. No matter how much I depend upon you for my answers, I still must make my own decisions.

Perhaps I can illustrate this aloneness paradox another way. Recall the times you have felt alone in the middle of a crowd. If you felt this separateness as pain, it was because you were not comfortable and loving with yourself. Instead, your mind was preoccupied with "What will they think of me?" "Will I find someone I know?" "Why do I feel so all alone?" In those circumstances, you had lost contact with the universal force; and when that happens, we forget who we truly are. That's why we feel pain.

To assuage the pain, we think it is necessary to gain others' approval. From this mistaken need, we change our act, hoping that someone—just anyone—will approve and befriend us so that we won't feel alone. We overlook the fact that—and here is that paradox again—we are, on the ultimate spiritual level, never alone. We are part of the one, the whole, and always connected with everything that is. Our troubles begin when we lose consciousness of this fact.

People never cease to be amazed when I tell them that they, as individuals, are the final authorities on everything in their lives. After all, who else can be the expert on your life? Who else can say what you feel and say what you want? You have, within yourself, all of the answers, and that is why you must learn to take charge of, and take full responsibility for, yourself. There is no other person, no place, no system, no philosophy, no church, no organization that knows more about *you* than *you* do.

Have you given up living because of what "they" would say about the way you lived? If you have, you sold yourself down the river, and it's time to stop doing that. There is a simple formula that will enable you to live any lifestyle you choose. And it works, if you are ready for it. Here it is: *As long as that which you do is ethical, as long as you do not want to hurt, steal, or take from another person, then the lifestyle you choose has to be good.*

I want you to think about that statement and make it your own. Then, if you wish, take it a step further. Determine the lifestyle you would choose if there were no obstacles at all. Don't worry if it sounds crazy or if it means that you should give up things and people who are in your life now. Just get very clear on what it is that you want. And, if you want others to join you in this lifestyle (whatever it is), write down the rules they would have to follow if they were to join you.

You can literally create a community of people who agree with you, if that's what you want; but you can't inflict or impose your views on others. Look at the people who first came to this country. In large part, they came because they didn't like the lifestyle, principally religious, they had in the Old Country. Of course, there were other pressures, economic and political, but they came here to set up a lifestyle in which they would be free to worship as they wished. Their problems began when they forgot their real reason for coming and began to insist that all others worship and live as they dictated. When we inflict our views on others, the social fabric, in home or community, rips apart.

What I'm saying is that, if you choose as your lifestyle a commune, a return to the farm, a move from the suburbs to the inner city, or whatever—so long as it does not violate the ethical formula given above—then, what others think is none of your business. People may want to live celibate lives, grow vegetables with love instead of fertilizer, do all kinds of things that you or I may find a little bit crazy, but so long as they don't violate the ethical formula, who are *we* to say that *they* are wrong? We can't say the lifestyle of others is wrong just because it doesn't match our pictures. I'm trying to illustrate that the reverse is equally true: Who is to say that the way *you* choose to live *your* life is wrong?

Another illustration is a woman who works for me. She is a recovered alcoholic and has three children who were certainly not raised according to the rules of *Good Housekeeping*. In fact, during the last two years of her drinking, she left the children alone night after night. Our conventional belief is that those kids should have grown up to be troublemakers, finding an early way to juvenile hall. Well, it didn't work that way. She quit drinking, got her life squared away, and the kids are fine, self-reliant achievers.

But she still doesn't raise them according to the rules. She doesn't always come home and fix dinner: she's still away from home a lot. But she encourages the kids to be independent and responsible. They're the prized neighborhood babysitters, trusted and respected by both peers and adults, get top grades in school, and are happy. Several people in her life continue to tell her she is doing the wrong thing; but when you look at the results, who's to say?

One reason this woman's family works is that they have all learned to be honest with one another. She tells them, frankly, that she hates to cook. So she buys the groceries, and they cook. Sometimes they complain that she doesn't spend enough time with them. They talk about her reasons for not spending more time at home—her job and volunteer work in Alcoholics Anonymous. She listens closely to what they have to say. Together they make whatever rearrangements are necessary for the living comfort of all concerned. Then, they move on to full participation in life. So what you think of her is none of her business, because her life—previously misspent—and the lives of her children are working.

Then, there is a friend who had a good job in real estate. As is often true in that business, his income went up and down like a roller coaster. He became tired of this feast-famine situation and one day, just quit, with no idea of what he would do next. Friends in the business told him he was crazy, but he quit, anyway, and took a menial job while he reflected on what he really wanted to do. Real estate friends continued to tempt him with good job offers, disapproving each time he turned them down. One day he realized that all of his life he had been drawn to writing. But where do you start? Particularly, with people around you telling you that a good way to starve is to become a writer. He found the pressures against him tremendous; but he stuck with his intention, once he had discovered it, and, sure enough, a writing job turned up. But it was with a volunteer organization, paid no money. Nevertheless, he was convinced the organization would pay him when he demonstrated his worth. So he turned his full attention to the volunteer job, was receiving a small salary in a short time, and within a year, was making a substantial wage. He was also able to take well-paid writing jobs on the side. He's now more comfortable than he has ever been, is making more money than he ever did in real estate, and best of all, loves what he does and is good at it. Had this man allowed what others thought to become *his business*, he would still be unhappy, unexpressed, and *in the wrong business!*

So, *what you think of me is none of my business!* I know that I am in charge of my life. I accept that I am my own best friend and the real authority on my own life. That does not mean that I don't love and support others, or that I won't listen to what they have to say to and about me. I know that I can learn from others, but I refuse to let others dump their negativism on me.

In some ways, our enemies are our best friends. We *can* learn from them if we don't let our personal feelings get in the way. We are not as likely to learn from our lovers, simply because they are apt to think we are super and need no improvement or growth. But we can listen to what others say; and if objectively it makes sense, we can simply apply it and move on. It's when we react with fear or defensively that we have a clue that something isn't right with us.

For example, when I feel very vulnerable, my children will take advantage of the situation. All my daughter has to say is, "We didn't have dinner tonight," and I plug right in. The truth is that she will walk miles for a tennis lesson or to see a boyfriend. So why can't she walk into the kitchen? But I tend to take it personally and feel guilty, which does neither of us any good. What she's really saying is that she misses me and wants to spend more time with me. It's when I notice the guilt in myself that I remember that my daughter and I can resolve our problem. Dinner's not the issue: she's just reflecting my own state of mind at the time.

Each of us needs to stand back and say: "What you think of me is none of my business." Each of us is the only authority on his or her own life; and if I let you push my buttons, we both lose. For then you manipulate rather than support me, and I've let you run my life, thus depriving myself of my own good.

I want you to look at yourself and say, "I had better accept more good for myself in my life, because it starts with me." Do you realize what would happen if each of us took the position of knowing, accepting, and loving ourselves? There would be no pain because it starts with each of us.

Accept that you are one with God and that you have the power to create your life exactly the way you want it. And remember: *What I think of you is none of your business.*

ACKNOWLEDGMENTS

It is customary in the writing of books for authors to acknowledge those who have aided them in their labors. I have been fortunate to receive the support of many in my living and in my writing, and I wish to use this space to thank Barbara Crawford and Adam Reich, my parents, for their willingness to create and love a new person; Suzanne Cole and Rebecca Cole, my children, for showing me that they are wise beyond me and for being my best friends; Guy Loraine for giving me my first opportunity to speak; Lloyd Tupper, Gene Graves, and Don McArt; my office staff for their continuing support on a daily basis; and my congregation for their love and encouragement.

Also deserving of my gratitude are Sarito, who refused to let me settle for mediocrity; Edith Hunio, whose amazing ability to organize freed me to do what I do best; Anne Wayman and Bill Glasgow, who worked diligently with me on this book; and Cindy and Charles Tillinghast, whose faith and support as publishers made it a reality.

I acknowledge the immeasurable contribution of all the people who have supported me as a person and as a teacher—including those who appeared to obstruct me—because, ultimately, everyone in our lives supports our spiritual enlightenment and personal magnificence.

Photo by Michael Bolger

Terry Cole-Whittaker is considered to be one of the premier inspirational and spiritual teachers and empowerment speakers in the world. Her Emmy-winning television ministry, *With Love, Rev. Terry*, aired on four hundred stations, reached millions, and inspired many to pursue a life of service, life coaching, spiritual teaching, and healing. Dr. Terry's pioneering work opened the door for a plethora of motivational speakers, bestselling authors, ministers, and leaders to come forth and succeed, and her ministry outreach and bestselling books made metaphysical teachings part of mainstream America. Her positive methods have reached tens of thousands through classes, seminars, workshops, counseling, TV, and radio.

CONNECT ONLINE

TerryColeWhittaker.com
🐦 TColeWhittaker